... that movie in your head

Guide to Improvising Stories on Video

David Shepherd

Gere Publishing, Shutesbury, Massachusetts

...that movie in your head

Guide to Improvising Stories on Video

by David Shepherd

Published by

Gere Publishing
113 Leonard Road
Shutesbury, Massachusetts 01072-9783

Orders@GerePublishing.com
www.GerePublshing.com

Cover design by Frederick Schneider/Grafis
Cover photography by Greg Caulton, www.stayintouch.org
Interior design by Claudia Gere, www.ClaudiaGereCo.com

Second Printing

LCCN 2003114354

ISBN 0-9743995-0-7

Printed in the United States of America

Contents

Preface

In 1952 at the University of Chicago's Reynold's Club, a dozen students are draped on a dusky stage. There is no set. The rumpled space resembles a Morning After. Inchmeal, action is emerging. Players lunge underneath the same pillows they've been sitting on. One crawls out to loft an object (imagined) into another group. Soldiers? A grenade loops back. A hit; I know because I hear a nasty cry. No dialog, just silhouettes moving around the injured man. Taunts from one trench to the other. Threats. Curses.

This location starts to dissolve. Bodies rise—high over the heels of dancing toes. Three bodies merge to create a hurdy-gurdy, cranking out celebration. Some dance, some stroll, some neck, some drink. A tone of ribaldry builds—it's a sleazy group at a country fair falling under the spell of music.

And still no direction! No barked signals. No whispered cues. No distortion to get laughs. I can't figure it out. Why is the group, without a visible leader, so creative, so comfortable? What's the secret? What's the gimmick?

The gimmick is Viola Spolin's games of transformation—introduced by Viola's son, Paul Sills. His students would transform all day, if there were time enough.

Five decades ago, Paul and I produced, with Charlie Jacobs, the first professional theatre of improvisation in America, Chicago COMPASS, with a new 70-minute show every week.

It was staffed by Mike Nichols and Elaine May, by Stiller and Meara, Barbara Harris, Severn Darden, and Shelley Berman, later by Alan Alda and Alan Arkin, and men who did both tech and improv: Roger Bowen and Andy Duncan.

COMPASS was the theatre that gave us not only European-style cabaret but also purely American elements—like the scenario play. This was a 40-minute story involving 6 to 8 players in the politics of work, love, family. It dealt with adoption, divorce, self-improvement, teen sexuality—whatever was brought to us by audience or cast.

Figure 1. Alan Alda improvising JFK while the audience plays the press. Carousel Theater, Cape Cod, Massachusetts, 1963.

The energy that launched COMPASS returned to me in the 90's. I found myself inventing scenarios, inviting friends over, coaching them while shooting them on video, editing in camera, and finally replaying the tape—all within 3 to 4 hours. Many offered a donation and returned month after month.

Paul Solomon took one of our tapes, "Shanty Queen," from home to home and led discussions about homelessness.

On the other hand, we discovered our tapes enraged the professional video producer: our framing was wrong, lighting uneven, sound weak, camera unsteady, focus soft, scenarios flimsy.

One expert told me the first thing I should do was hire him at $1000 a day. Another said every one of our takes should be shot 5 times—from different angles—and assembled in edit. (We edit very little in the studio.)

According to them, our organic stories, our uncomedic improvisation, our edits in camera, our choice of costume, and our gratifyingly quick pace have no value. What has value to them is the Hollywood movie, which costs $10,000/minute, or the TV commercial, which costs a lot more.

To them the people of value are not those eager to interact and express some new part of themselves but those who risk millions to produce a feature that may bring them a profit in a foreign market.

Of course scripted video movies have been around for decades—made usually by professionals. What's new is improvising them so fast that the cast, often nonprofessional, can see what it has made in a day or two.

To do that we use not film but video, we improvise action, and we edit in camera. Since nonprofessionals can play roles similar to the ones they play in real life, they bring a lot of reality to our short movies.

We don't spend time writing and rewriting a story, typing and revising a script. Often the group doesn't know what its story will be until it meets on the day before the shoot. What comes out of the group's brainstorm is not frozen dialog. It's a scenario launched into video by players who know their roles and express them sharply—with feeling.

The root of our work, which enables us to create short videos in days or hours, is improvisation. It also enables you to create music, poetry, and comedy without memorizing notes or lines. *Improvisation* is the basic technology of our work.

Not too long ago, we pushed improv, week after week, into another area—editing, which is traditionally done solo. In East Hampton, New York, I invited parishioners from my church to screen source footage of "I Can't Get No..." at Pizza n' Things. I gave them a polling sheet covering 40 interviews and 7 scenes. They checked off what they liked best. Their notes went to our editor, so he was no longer talking to himself.

My staff was horrified: "An editor," they claimed, "must work alone under your direction." (This would be "Improv for Two.") But the story-line taste of Carol, Hugh, Terry, Matt, Sabina, Vic, Nancy, and others was closer to the taste of those who bought the video cassette than mine. Our pollsters were not squeezed into a dark editing suite with space for only one chair. They were nine people relating at their convenience to about an hour of footage that wanted to be boiled down to 28 minutes for Channel 70.

Now I want to bring off improv movies—staffed by people like you who are scanning these words at this moment. Before going to the story of how I was inoculated for life by improv, let me say: I don't mind if you mislay this book or give it away. I care only that you believe you can produce your own video movie—and do it. I tell participants at the end of our screenings: "It doesn't really matter what happens to this footage. It's your experience that's important, and you had that before the screening."

Now we predict not only that you end up with a cassette (to put in your library), but also that

- you can have the unique experience of
  — telling your story
  — shaping your role
  — playing your scene
  — screening your movie
  — shaping it in edit
- and this experience will stay with you the rest of your life.

David Shepherd

Start Your Group

So why should I make my own movie? Because it's now possible, whereas before it was not. Just like poetry slams, the Internet, women CEOs, karaoke. Once upon a time, there was no karaoke. Now there is karaoke. Making your own movie is similar:

- it's fun
- it's demanding
- it's social
- it builds skills
- it expresses what your group has to say

People create their own community theatre, dance group, debating club, garage band, opera company...But is theatre, dance, debate, jazz, or opera the dominant medium today? No, movies are. Not documentary movies, dance movies or abstract movies, but narratives.

Once a week billions of people watch one or two stories on film. They are constructed at great expense in Hollywood, Cinecitta, Bombay, and elsewhere. The flow of films now moves one way only, from supplier to you. Meanwhile billions flow from all of you to the supplier—through movie complexes.

Outside of Hollywood do movies really have to cost so many millions? Shouldn't you be able to make a movie for a fraction of the current price and see it travel from consumer to consumer or friend to friend?

Why haven't movie lovers, until recently, made their own movies? Because there are very few models. There's very little guidance—books that say, "Pick up your camcorder and do this."

We offer these pages as proof that you can make your own movie. A story you produce on videotape may not sell Hollywood or the networks. But it can interest your children, parents, neighbors, classmates, fellow employees, plus a festival or two.

You'll read how improvisation generates great, believable performances and how video can capture and edit them for cable station & video store, for festival & home.

As of 2006, your video piece can appear on line at the Web site: www.groupcreativityproject.com. Let us know about your piece at groupcreativity@charter.net.

MOVIExperience

This is more than a book that you're holding. This guide contains a program called MOVIExperience that is transforming as you read. After years of experiments, we're just beginning to pin down the experience of a video movie.

- It comes together so rapidly that you get to make many instantaneous decisions—about story, its meaning, its location, who's in the cast.
- It offers you a chance to play, watch, comment, and even do tech.
- It assures you of an immediate screening of your creation.
- You can get a dupe of the edited tape by mail—within days.

Now you can bring off improv movies—staffed by friends like you who are scanning these words at this moment. To see this daring new art form for yourself, go to your video store and rent:

This is Spinal Tap, Waiting for Guffman, Best in Show, A Mighty Wind, The Blair Witch Project, Magnolia, The Anniversary Party, the works of John Cassavetes; and more are being released this year.

You'll read a dozen insights into how we do what we do by the people we've worked with in:

- Bedford, PA
- Chelsea, NYC, NY
- Chicago, IL
- Des Moines, IA
- East Hampton, NY
- Los Angeles, CA

- Northampton, MA
- NYC, NY
- Phoenix, AZ
- Tribeca, NYC, NY
- Woodbridge, NJ
- and more...

We try to guarantee, from casting to screening, that everybody has a good time.

Using This Guide

There isn't any reason one or two people can't make a movie using the improv techniques in this book, but it is really geared for groups, for instance:

- a parent with children and their friends who like to play games
- a teacher and students in video, social studies, or creative writing classes
- a social action group that has an important story for cable
- an improv club that's ready to branch out to video
- readers of consumer video magazines or technical publications
- hobbyists, the curious, and people about to buy equipment
- consumers who own equipment and want to use it but don't know which closet it's in

Glossary

A glossary at the end defines terms used in this book as well as other terms used in the moviemaking world you should know.

Action

Readers are encouraged to put down the book, get out their camcorders, and do the exercises in this guide. Throughout this book, you'll see these signs:

⌘ **Try It! Play a game using new techniques or complete a sample exercise to show what you know.**

 Shoot It! Either give your camcorder to the players or try a new technique described in the book.

√ **A checklist to help you remember what you need to know.**

You'll also find Fast Lane, a boxed column at the beginning of some chapters to help you jump right into moviemaking.

This is a guide, not a step-by-step formula. Making a movie doesn't require reading this book from beginning to end. In fact, the book encourages you to pick up your camera often and experiment.

The Fast Lane sidebars let you experience moviemaking with very little reading. You can skip through the book and accelerate your movie experience. Later, read the rest of the book at your leisure. The first five chapters give you the basics for getting started, and the later chapters build on your knowledge of the first five.

Staffing Your Group

Don't read this guide alone! First find a few friends likely to work with you because they know equipment, tell tall stories or enjoy being creative. Then read it together—while doing the activities in each chapter, such as:

- Coach's Signals
- improv games
- question & answer exercises

You'll get much more out of discussing your movie with friends, as you activate your equipment, than turning these pages alone. You've probably picked out at least one person already.

⌘ Get a moviemaking friend

Look for someone who:

- you can support and
- supports you
- you can argue with
- can carry equipment and clean up
- can think through a problem
- understands people's behavior and
- can work with a group

I've been lucky in my choice of partners. One ex-partner stars on Canadian TV. One's an industrial trainer. One runs a bicoastal business, and another is using MOVIExperience to develop self-esteem in teenage girls.

After you have a friend enrolled, you'll need to complete your staff. People can take on multiple roles; just make sure you staff all roles. Here are the roles you'll see mentioned through the guide:

Camcorder Operator

The Camcorder Operator, also called the Camera Operator, carries camcorder, tripod, batteries & blank cassettes. Is responsible for other equipment: battery charger, microphones, lights, extension cords, 2 to 3 adapters, reflector board, lenses, filters. Labels tape religiously. Can also train an assistant.

Figure 2. Nikhil Melnuchuk and Charlotte de Vries. Photo credit: Claudia Gere

The Camera Operator shoots steady while walking, positions and adjusts lighting, gets up high or down low, goes macro (extreme close-up) uses *white balance,* shoots traveling footage from car or boat, uses fade & other effects, screens tape in the eyepiece with a headset.

The Operator knows how many seconds of tape the camcorder erases when it records from the OFF position or from PAUSE. Operators rewind to the beginning of the last take in order to record over it. They supervise helpers who upgrade a location, plug in spotlights or a light kit, use a boom or a lavaliere mic, position a light board. Keep camcorder dry during rainy shoots and protect it from sand on the beach.

Coach

The Coach shoots in an emergency and can take over the job of Project Manager or Experience Host. Pays attention to players' energy—both on location and off. Gathers games that warm up players and take away their reliance on talk. Encourages players to make physical contact, express feeling, tag, sing.

Keeps the ending of each scene open (so players either don't know what the ending is or have options to reach a fixed ending). At the Brainstorm makes sure the scenario chosen makes sense and can be performed. With an Assistant Coach, tweaks the scenario to improve continuity.

Chooses Coach's Signals that reduce wordiness, enlarge feeling, vary rhythm. Knows where to remove a Coach's Signal and trust players to work without games. Is aware when continuity breaks and repairs it by using a Bridge or reshooting the scene.

Trains an Assistant to Coach the Bridge players and Crowd players so they know they're adding something valuable to the movie. Is willing to make cast changes even though a player objects. If a player leaves a shoot, quickly makes changes in scenario or cast and continues.

Changes a location to strengthen the scene. Assistant Coach makes sure players use costume pieces whenever they go on camera. Runs Warm-Ups whenever players lose energy. Makes sure each player is wearing clothes that make a statement and is using props that focus the improv.

Project Manager

Project Manager can shoot in an emergency or take the jobs of Experience Host or Coach. Carries promo tapes and reprints about the group's work. Explains MOVIExperience to friends and strangers. Adapts the program to new clients—in homes, businesses, schools, and elsewhere. Makes staff changes that enable the staff to play very small or very large groups. Supervises training of new staff and volunteers.

Reaches out for volunteers; finds schools, cable stations and production companies where volunteers can apply for future jobs. Prepares talent releases and has them signed by the cast (and by parents of young kids).

The Project Manager arranges for tape editing to remove glitches and add Titles and Credits. With help finds film festivals where MOVIExperience tapes may be screened. Contacts people likely to donate to a shoot or to editing costs, festival fees, and overhead. Knows which businesses are patronized by members of the group and requests a donation from them.

If the shoot is short, asks players for a fee of $10 to $50 (depending on whether the player wants a dupe). Estimates number of dupes to be made by a volunteer or by a dupe house. Has a cassette cover designed. Places a tape and poster in video rental stores to attract customers to the next video movie.

With staff evaluates each shoot to understand how the group is growing. Keeps a file of photographers willing to cover shoots, brainstorms, and screenings. Reaches out to the press and sets up interviews with staff or cast.

Files permissions, source tapes, masters, dupes, and newsprint in a safe location.

Experience Host

Prepares snacks, drinks, seating, and whatever else adds to the comfort of participants. Sets up a VCR & monitor to screen tapes that were recently shot. Gives out name tags and sheets of Frequently Asked Questions. Takes names and addresses while answering other questions. Notices which participants know video, which are eager or shy (and lets other staff know). Collects donations or fees to cover the production costs. Explains to participants what happens at a typical MOVIExperience.

Figure 3. Candace runs Brainstorm session on New York's Lower East Side. The community has come out for her story, "Getting Off," which is about drugs and saying no to temptation. Excitement in the group has peaked. Photo credit: Hronn Axelsdottir.

When participants don't understand, explains in detail. Where necessary asks whoever is running the shoot to be clearer. Pays attention to the temperature of the room and to irritations that prevent participants from enjoying themselves.

- Offers jobs that participants can handle: lights, sound, storyboard, continuity, costumes, props, makeup, and so on. Demonstrates these jobs. Arranges for participants to shoot tape #2 either on camera #1 or on camera #2. Suggests short video goals, such as:
- "Give these new players a Screen Test."
- "Shoot that horizon off a tripod while this player runs across."
- "Circle around this couple as they walk in the mall."

To promote another MOVIExperience, asks participants what special location they'd like to visit, what stories they'd like to tell.

Introduces people to each other when they share something (e.g., they live close to each other or have the same occupation or hobby). Allows bystanders to just sit and watch the shoot.

Players

A player is a person who likes games, who would rather play and lose than not play at all. A player likes the risk of not knowing what the outcome of a scene will be. A player is interested in meeting new-comers—simply because they are different.

A player enjoys exploring new behavior and is intrigued by different experiences. For instance, a player finds it rewarding to play a parent or grandparent, a cop or a female exec. Our video improvisation games justify reaching out, taking chances, meeting surprises, learning about who we would be if we weren't who we are.

In a group you can spot players by the way they keep changing their relationship to each other. They test who they are by making ironic comments, jumping into different characters, feeling out different situations. They make surprising statements, and we have to be able to tell which are real and which are jokes.

Other group members can play straight men and women to the leading players. They are the surgeon ready to operate, or the mechanic ready to tell the player what is the matter with their car. These performers look not for what they have never known, but what they know cold.

Crew

Some participants want to enjoy the experience without going on camera. Others want it all—to play one or two roles and hold down a crew position, too.

Anyone who doesn't want to be on camera can be Tech: Production Asst, Continuity, Refreshments, Documentation, Lights, Grip, Sound, Scenario, Host, Hostess, Publicity, Gofer, Makeup, Location Scout.

Assistant Camera

A second camera can be used to make a tape that's shown before the story tape at the screening. Participants take the job of Assistant Camera Person, shooting selectively—only one minute out of 10.

Their camera experience gives the cast quick views of Brainstorm, Casting, Warm-Ups, the shoot, and the personal interaction of participants. This documenting footage is sometimes more interesting than the movie.

We can also ask Camera #2 to shoot improvs that complement the main story. When we have a large number of 'participants, Camera #2 can involve players who didn't get speaking roles.

Assistant Coach

The Assistant Coach can prepare scenes parallel to the story so they can be shot. In "Obsession," for instance, Michael shot all the players one after another talking about whatever obsessed them. An Assistant Coach would immediately sketch these feelings as improvs lasting only a few seconds each to develop their confidences into a series of short scenes.

Choosing Interesting Locations

Even without people in it, a location can be physically dynamic:

- clouds plunge the earth into shadow or sun;
- every 30 seconds chimes clank;
- bugs skid across a marshy pond.

A location at dawn will work differently for you than the same space at dusk or at midnight. To the camera, these are three different locations.

As a player, you're automatically a Location Scout. You're expected to come up with lots of quirky, splendid, practical, extraordinary, sordid, surprising, threatening, romantic... locations. So start collecting a few!

Unlike a stage set, which is usually hand built and static, the movie locations that we need are real. Choose locations that are already interesting (ski slope or amusement park). Shoot when there's maximum activity. For instance, shoot plumbers carrying pipe as a wheelchair passes behind them or shoot as a teenager lifts a giggling baby into the air.

⌘ Where would you locate a scene about a daughter leaving her parents?	⌘ Where would you get the most interesting scene with a coach and player?
▪ on a parched backyard?	▪ in a locker room?
▪ in a pet store?	▪ in the coach's office?
▪ before a waterfall?	▪ at a pin ball machine?
▪ in a breakfast nook?	▪ in the front seat of a car?
▪ in a pickup truck?	▪ walking on the campus?

Answers: I'd give the daughter a spade to dig up the backyard and plant a bush. For the basketball scene I'd take the office, where the coach has status, or the pinball machine, where the player has status.

Activating Uninteresting Locations

Look how you can upgrade any boring location by activating it.

- typical kitchen—Hold a burning cigarette in front of the players and shoot through the plume of smoke.
- the usual office—Off camera put a salesman making a sale by phone.
- in an ordinary garden—A red frisbee sails back and forth above the hedge next door.
- lifeless bedroom—Add an audio dimension; put players outside in the alley shouting "go fetch" to a barking dog.
- standard bathroom—The tub is overflowing, and biker magazines are scattered on the sink.
- usual tavern—Balloons bounce in and out of a stream of air from a fan.
- listless highway—Add a beat-up car parked at an angle with one door open and streamers flapping off the bumper.
- department store—Suspicious shoppers sniff at a perfume sample.
- conventional park—Teens run by passing a football back and forth.
- any restaurant—Hungry customers wave in vain for the menu.
- empty beach—A volleyball game starts on a distant dune— loud and serious.

⌘ **Here are some blah locations—the kind you might have to accept for your shoot. How would you activate each one?**

▪ a country porch	▪ accountant's office
▪ back alley	▪ basement
▪ bookstore	▪ master bedroom

Choosing Locations That Encourage Play

The edge of the surf, for instance, is a location that suggests great activities:

- building a sand castle
- writing a message for someone in wet sand
- burying a willing player to the neck in dry sand

Figure 4. Amagansett Main Beach—sandcastle setting for "How to Tell If You're in the Hamptons" (1993). Photo credit: Author.

Imagine what can be done with a wall mirror—it sucks the player in—to examine a pimple, pull a wild hair, tie a tie, comb down a curl....

⌘ **Your turn: add your playful locations to ours.**

▪ the first hole on a golf course	Add yours here:
▪ in thick bramble	▪ _____
▪ at a subway turnstile	▪ _____
▪ on a ladder to a tree house	▪ _____
▪ dropping water balloons off a balcony	▪ _____
▪ ocean waves and barking dog	▪ _____

Using Foreground and Background

Allow players to pass in front of the camera briefly; their appearance makes the scene more lifelike, even if their bodies blur. Pedestrians who pass behind the action can be useful if you tell them what to do—read the paper, point at the sky, gesticulate as they tell jokes, feed the pigeons, argue.

Figure 5. Cafe Black Sheep: sidewalk chairs at 8:00 a.m., soon to be filled by students for "How to Tell If You're at UMass" (2001).

⌘ **Planning a shoot**

Talk over locations you'd like to use in your movie, for instance:

surfing—Would you shoot while wading or from a sand dune?

women boxers—What seat would give the best viewpoint?

hospital patients—What time of day, what lighting, what kind of microphone?

kindergarten—How near the floor can you get, using which zooms and pans?

beauty parlor—Who would you put a lavaliere microphone on?

warehouse—Do you prefer industrial lighting or spots, what wattage?

park—At what time of day will you get the right strollers in the background?

amphitheatre—Who do you want speaking, on what issue?

car accident—From what angle will it not look fake?

If your discussion leads to theme and story, go with it. Jot it down. Keep a collection of stories that stay in your head. Share some with friends. Ask them to be in your movie.

Collect Your Locations on One Video

Before your scenario brainstorming session, shoot a Locations tape to show the cast a couple of dozen favorite (or secret) places where scenes can be shot. None should be more than a five-minute walk from Home Base.

If there's an important prop in the location—such as a laptop computer or a vase of iris—do a short cutaway to remind the editor it is there—waiting to be used.

Bring a portable boombox and cassettes so you can flavor each location with music, news, or radio talk. If you limit each location shot to 10 seconds, two dozen locations will take 4 minutes to screen.

See how valuable your tape will be! First of all, it will keep brainstormers from choosing a story that can't be shot at this time and place. Students of mine once chose a cabin surrounded by snow for a scene. But it was July! On the stage you can pretend you're shivering and snowed in. In movies the viewer wants to see real icicles in close-up—with falling snow drifting against the front door.

Your tape will also remind the cast of little known locations they forgot—and of great locations that you missed. It will put story ideas into heads and suggest how action can flow—from racetrack to living room or from living room to racetrack.

≡✦➤ Shooting your location video

Ask a few players to go along and enliven each location, or help shoot, for instance:

location—medium shot of an empty counter for 2 seconds

   action—Customers rush in and fill all seats.

location—low shot of a cemetery from grass level

   action—Two players step over the camera and stroll off, holding hands.

location—long shot of empty railroad station platform

   action—A commuter rushes on, checks his watch, looks up the tracks, checks his watch again.

location—horizon of vast field: using tripod, zoom in slowly

   action—Farm workers gesticulate, arguing at top volume.

location—kitchen during party: shoot tight for character .

   action—Guests appear bored, amused, cynical, sensual, sleepy.

location—executive office: shoot from behind in-box for mail

   action—Hands drop mail into in-box or take it from out-box.

location—crossroads: tight shot from ground level close to traffic so tires of passing cars look huge;

   action—On opposite side of street pedestrians pass a hitchhiker.

Figure 6. Shelburne Falls: rocks, potholes and cascades for "I'm Getting Seven Million" (1998).

The first step into a MOVIExperience is savoring possible locations, comparing them. Give participants the feeling that their knowledge of the community and their smart choices can make the movie a hit. You are not the final word; the group is.

⌘ Dealing with locations

- Pick 3 locations at noon; imagine 3 scenes you could shoot there; what activity or prop is available to the cast in each location?
- Change the time to midnight; how do your scenes change; now what activity would be available to each cast?
- Pick one location and change it 3 times—by changing only sound and lighting; invent three scenes that would work there.
- Keep these locations the same, but change the cast; what happens now?

You're Short of Time on a Shoot?

In a big living room you may have fireplace, glass doors, a coffee table setting, closet, armchair, desk. Shoot tight, close blinds, adjust lights, and add sound. Each one of these locations can appear to be a separate place. Even a buzzer can be a location—if you shoot the finger that touches it in an extreme close-up.

Figure 7. One extensive location can hold a dozen separable locations—locating all close to each other. So one Production Assistant is setting up for the pond while another is preparing the picnic only a dozen yards away. Illustration by Anita Fritz.

You Ran out of Locations?

Don't be surprised. Our Home Base is usually a public place that has no homey settings or a home with no public settings. But most scenarios need office *and* beach, mall *and* hearth, loading dock *and* tomato patch.

You can do a corporate scene on a suburban street; shoot players from below so we see only their props—clipboard or blueprint—against the sky. To do a home scene inside a corporation, place a cutting board with onions, for instance, on a table in a corner and a family picture on the wall behind. Or shoot monologs that are extreme close-ups so the background fades out of the picture.

Figure 8. NYC, St. Marks Place: David Haber and Robin Salant improvise old friends meeting by accident at a bar (1990). Photo credit: Jody Butters.

Players need to breathe—rather than squeeze themselves into the same old living room, kitchen, or bedroom. They want to visit exciting places that will suggest exciting scenarios. If you make this possible, they'll put more energy into the shoot.

√ Checklist for a location

what activities are possible—In a kitchen, a stained and dirty table demands to be cleaned. In a warehouse, an enormous box offers flat space for a card game. In a field, 4-leaf clovers beg to be picked.... On the other hand, a stalled elevator or street corner offers very little.

power—When your battery needs to be recharged, are there 110-volt outlets? How long should your extension cord be if you plan to shoot using AC power?

sound interference—Is there a fan, air conditioner, refrigerator or some other constant noise; can it be eliminated while you shoot?

lights—When you come back to do the shoot, will clamp-on spots be needed or a light kit? If you're relying on sputtering neon, do a test recording before the shoot.

crowd control—What kind of people (bar customers, kids, tourists) are you likely to get during the shoot? Should you risk putting them on camera? Do you need them to sign talent releases?

360 degrees—Does the location allow a cameraperson to do a long pan? To climb up and shoot down? Try it.

changes—At the shoot, will a location prove to be different from when you first scouted it—light, sounds, traffic, people...?

availability—Will this wonderful space still be available when you need it?

2 Your Screen Test Replayed

A Screen Test is a glance—on video—at the potential of a player. Your Locations tape has shown where you can make your movie. Your Screen Test tape will show who's coming out for it.

Know the Players

Step up to the camcorder and show you're committing yourself to the movie. You're willing to let the camera frame you, hug you, flatter you. You're willing to answer questions, talk up, move to directions. You're ready to play—with old friends or strangers.

You're ready to make a decision: either play a character you know cold, like your teacher in sixth grade. Or play yourself—whether you hold a lasso in your gloved hand or a sterile hypodermic in your scrubbed fingers. Just be yourself—as warden or Olympic star, beautician or cosmonaut. And if you don't understand what you're expected to do, assume that this is your first day on the job, and you're doing the best you can.

Richard Romboletti, for instance, arrived at a MOVIExperience carrying a robe and a heavy cross. He wanted to know what it would be like to be a priest—among flaming liberals and people with problems that needed his attention. He got quite a few takers, and he discovered what it was to work in the career that he passed up in his teens.

Why Do a Screen Test?

Suppose everybody already knows all the players; then why do Screen Tests? Because, it's part of the experience of making a movie. From childhood people dream of the Hollywood audition. Now they can have one on their home turf. Catch them in any quiet place—on a roof, after work, in a park. If passing co-workers or family members get curious, recruit them as players.

Is the final cassette more important than the *experience* your group has? No. The way we designed it, our improv movie should be shaped by its players. They are in on every big decision—from scouting locations to choosing which footage to edit or dupe.

Tell players: "Doing your own Screen Test is not enough. You should also see everybody else's Screen Test. Get into the experience of Casting Director; choose players for parts and parts for players."

Doing the Super Self

Camera Operator, ask a player to walk around while talking. Camera circles the body and shoots profile, hands, feet. Ask, for instance:

- "What's your name?"
- "Talk three times louder, please?"
- "Thank you. Where do you come from?" By now the player's posture, voice, rhythm, gait, personality are clear.
- "Show us more of yourself. More. Be your Super Self!"
- "Walk faster (or slower); put your chin higher (lower); talk louder (softer)...Show us more feeling. Good."
- "As your Super Self, what part do you want to play in our movie?"
- "What do you want to be doing in that part? Give us a sample. Say something you'd say in that part."

This Screen Test takes about 45 seconds. Shoot a couple dozen people, and the tape takes 20 minutes to review.

Other Self

If you have a small cast, take more time with each player. Encourage each to play some person they are not—an Other Self. A shy person may have wanted for years to play a big shot. A finicky person may have wanted to play a slob, a tight person—loose, a cynic—an optimist. Now's their chance.

This longer Screen Test takes a minute or more. Play the tape back just before the Brainstorm, so storytellers know who they have to work with.

Letting Participant Shoot

To assure participants of a more complete experience, let them use the camcorder.

 **Camcorder Operator**

First find out if they can use the zoom and let them go. Attach the camera's carrying strap around their wrist.

Reshoot every candidate yourself in your style and at your minimum length so the tape stays short and segments can easily be compared.

Reviewing the Screen Tests

Once your Screen Test tape is finished, you can sit down to a feast. Across the monitor will pass all the talent you've assembled—to be savored, critiqued, compared.

Figure 9. Alsha Mable and Troy McDonald review tape for "La Gentrification de Pilsen."

Weak spot? Is there a certain age or type that's missing from the tape? Now's the time for your players to reach out, make a phone call. Now's the time to ask, before rushing into a Brainstorm, what kind of a movie can we make?

⌘ What kind of movie?	
▪ comedy	List your ideas:
▪ fantasy	———————————
▪ drama	———————————
▪ scrapbook nostalgia	———————————
▪ satire	———————————

How about farce, mystery, heavy action? No, it's too hard to improvise. You can't handle clever dialogue and misleading cues without a script and rehearsal. As for violence, you can decide to show a murdered character, but your viewers probably will not buy it.

Ask Brainstormers to talk up whenever they see something they like on the Screen Test tape. Keep things informal, responsive, and fun.

"It's better to put out a so-so MOVIExperience at which people have a good time, than a perfect one at which everyone is miserable."

—Terry Mollner

3 Brainstorm Your Scenario

Brainstorming is used to find solutions when no expert is around. Like the children's game "Simon Says," a well-run Brainstorm reduces many options to one—in seconds.

Keep your Locations tape running on a monitor that the cast can see, then the Screen Test tape, at low volume. Sit in a circle. The leader starts, saying exactly what's needed, for instance, a "story for 25 people that can be shot at locations 5 minutes from here." Going from player to player, others give their ideas.

- Voice the first *theme* that comes to you. No matter how dumb it seems to you, somebody else may fly with it. Or offer a *situation* that enlarges on a theme. For instance if the theme is *pride*, the situation could be *getting a big compliment from a person you barely know.*
- Rather than going off on your own tangent, build off the idea that came before you.
- No matter how crazy somebody's suggestion is—don't put it down
- Keep a list of all suggestions; pass this job person-to-person.

After an hour or less, you'll hold a shaggy list of at least two dozen suggestions. Read them aloud; you'll get laughs. Someone list a dozen on a chalkboard or newsprint. Voting raises the energy of the group because members now have to make decisions fast.

When I'm the leader, I tell participants they each have two votes. Read the list a second time, putting checks before every suggestion that gets a vote. Underline three or four winners. Discuss whether you have the locations & players to shoot them. One participant advances or rewinds the videotape so all can see what's available.

This time when I read the list of winners, each participant has only one vote. I find they usually cast it very carefully.

What's Happening?

The group is finding a solution that draws from the creativity of many people. Nobody can complain they've been left out.

Figure 10. A beautiful cast, but I wouldn't try to pull a scenario out of the group. It's too big. Divide it into teams of 3 to 4 players. "I'm Getting 7 Million" (1998). Photo credit:: Author

Brainstorming shows participants not only how to respect each other but also how any opinion can be woven into the movie. At the shoot you will see few participants asking themselves why they came out for your program. They have hooked themselves. They've become a vital part of the process.

- If at the screening people comment that the theme is weak, point out *they are the ones who chose it.*
- As Project Manager or Coach, do you disagree with the group's choice? Then say so.
- Does the story make sense, for instance? If not, can it be revised?
- Is it violent? Erotic? Is it based on cliché characters & formula plot?
- Will it be acceptable to the sponsor of the program? To cable viewers?
- Can the main parts be played by people who are present? Can you reach enough women, men, and children to fill the cast?
- Are there parts for people who want to play nonverbally? For people who may show up late?

If you're taking on too much, propose a simpler project.

⌘ Suggestions for a simpler project

- Shoot key scenes from the scenario.
- Shoot scenes about the theme but not the whole story.
- Shoot scenes between players who know each other well.
- Shoot monologs to audience suggestions.
- Shoot favorite games or Coach's Signals.
- Pair up and suggest 2 characters plus a location for each pair to play in.
- Have a party and record opinions, conversations, and role plays.

"MOVIExperience works best with people who know each other, or people who get to know each other before the shoot."

—Joan Carlson

Fitting Story, Cast, and Locations

If it's raining, and your locations are all in one house, your story can't be about a trip to the Grand Canyon. If your cast is all women and girls, your story can't be about pro football.

Say you come up with a story about a marriage between a conservative minister and a young urban anthropologist. The story has mystery, tension, twists & peaks plus a great resolution. You decide to do it. But first of all, how's the fit?

These locations have been offered, but do they frame the ghetto scenes you imagine?

⌘ Fitting locations to the scene	
Given locations	Imagined scenes
▪ below stained glass windows	▪ teen hangout
▪ soup kitchen	▪ computer at GED class
▪ attic bedroom	▪ cars racing at midnight
▪ bath	▪ college library

Answers: Your story can't be played in these locations! Get others. And who in your group can play out the story?

⌘ Fitting players to the scene		
Story roles	Available cast	Match: Yes/No
▪ deacon 35 years old	four 10-year-olds	____
▪ her 60-year-old boyfriend	3 hardware workers	____
▪ jet-set graduate students	male cashier—50	____
▪ minister's mom and dad	22-year-old female dancer	____
▪ 70-year-old expert on poison	30-year-old ex-actor	____

Answer: you don't have the right people to tell your story. By moving the Home Base you can get new locations, but you can't trade in your players. This story simply doesn't fit what you've been given. Use your second- or third-choice story.

If you plan to adjust this location and reshape that one, you may get into big trouble: viewers will not believe you. A word about belief and disbelief:

Movie buffs don't suspend disbelief. In fact, they're eager to catch mistakes. In movies a player cannot say, "There's bees under yonder porch." The Location Scout can't ask us to pretend there are bees. We must see the bees. And hear the swarm. That's why Story must match Locations and Cast as closely as possible.

Documenting the Experience

Camcorder Operator, here's your chance to document, in a 5- to 10-minute tape, key decisions that shape the project.

 Shooting a documentation tape

Shoot 1 minute for every 20, so a 2- to 3-hour session boils down to 6 to 9 minutes.

- It can show the importance of friends who were active in the Brainstorm but may not appear on the movie tape.
- It can also be played during the shoot when players get restless waiting to go on camera.
- It even serves as an evaluation that shows:

  □ This is what we discarded.

  □ This is what we discussed.

  □ This is what we went with.

Watch a Brainstorm Come up with a Scenario

Here's the strategy we used with a dozen employees of an electronics firm:

Day 1, Nancy meets two execs to find out what value our session will have for them. They're interested in learning more about their people's behavior outside the workplace. The CEO remarks, "there's no use spending thousands to hire people and not spending a dime to find out who they are." (This company is expanding, sending out its strongest employees to run new stores.)

Day 5, Izzy and David join Nancy to plan the session. We decide that when Nancy meets half a dozen employees at the 3-hour Brainstorm Day 12, she will:

- generate a bunch of themes quickly, such as Teamwork, Courage...
- ask which parts each employee wants to play.

Nancy's Brainstorm produces a very rough scenario that imitates TV. It features the theft of a lotto prize ($500), a husband buying his wife's murder and a woman chasing men through a building while carving the air with a knife. Nancy asks:

"Do we really have the Characters to fit this story?" (maybe)

"Do we have the Locations we need to shoot?" (yes)

"Is this really what we want to say?" (no)

"So what do we do?"

Working with employees, three of us build three stories—one about a dissatisfied step-daughter, one about the carving knife, and one about the police. We splice story lines until the scenario can be shot under the title: "Get Used to It." I coach while Izzy prepares the cast. He facilitates a debriefing later. Employees like what they see: everyone orders a dupe.

Nancy learns: if you meet a monster problem, instead of manfully wrestling it to the ground, just ask whoever is standing by, "What should we do?" That one question saves a lot of grief. And it allows players to experience the experience part of MOVIExperience.

Pre-Briefing

There's another way to tap the feelings of the cast a moment before production. It's called Pre-briefing. Ask players to imagine it's after the shoot and say what happened over the last hours.

When we did this before shooting "Shades of Leaving," we got a range of responses—from paranoia to joy. Dee said he was sorry a pedestrian was run over by our trucks, while Christine was amazed how one actor managed to fly up into the air and disappear.

You can control responses by narrowing the question: "Did you like the shoot?" or "Want to do another movie?" These questions encourage Yes/No answers about a movie to come.

4 Discover Your Cast

Character

Explore characters that may come up in a scenario. For instance, make a pack of cards. On one face it says father, on the other grandpa. On one face it says aunt, on the other little sister. Or teacher and principal, mafiosa and hacker...

When a person takes a card, they can choose to act like one or the other of the two characters. Give them a time limit—a minute or less.

To sharpen their focus, hand players a prop, such as a fingernail clipper or a newspaper.

Find out what newcomers to improv will feel when given a part to play at your next movie session.

At the Brainstorm, players have asserted themselves, backed down, joked, giggled. You know who's shy, goofy, boastful, helpful, angry, boring, snobbish.

You've heard participants speak loud or soft, fast or slow—with or without an accent. You've watched their body language (and they've watched yours) while you get hunches about some of them: this one is the rebellious type, this one protective, this one hard as steel. It's all on the Screen Test tape.

Which players would play well with each other? You sense this player as Teacher would spark that one as Clown; this Rebel would jog that Expert; this Babysitter would bounce off that Spoiled kid.

Can this 16-year-old play a 30-year-old? If your first choice scenario can't be played by this group, look at your second choice. Or shoot an anthology of short scenes that *can* be cast.

In casting, how will your experience differ from Hollywood? There, a Casting Director, who knows thousands of talents, negotiates with a first choice, then a second... until someone accepts an offer.

Here you're limited to using those in the group, but you can probe their ability to express feeling and play character. You can discover which ones are comfortable playing parts close to them and which prefer parts that are far away.

The ones with a knack for impersonation can give you an impression of whatever Stock Handler, Real Estate Agent, or Cabbie they've seen in action recently. Be ready for some surprises.

Surprises in Iowa

Long before we visited two high schools in Iowa, they mailed us Screen Tests of 50 kids. Eagerly we ripped open the package. But the kids on tape looked and sounded similar—as if they came from one big, bland family. (Actually, the camera had robbed them of personality.) We were worried.

At Des Moines airport, however, people were assertive, dependable, humorous. And at the Brainstorm the most off-beat suggestions came from Kathy—a teacher! The bland kids soon took the ball and ran with it.

A boy who had a reputation of being silent suggested that a federal agency paid a teenager $10,000 to wear a device in his brain. The agency was able to turn him into a terrorist at will. Pure Sci-Fi.

Other scenes attacked nerds, eggheads, showoffs, fame-seekers.

We had been dealt a full deck of strong opinions. And best of all, the kids already knew who they wanted to play. We avoided the risk of putting somebody we didn't know into the wrong part.

Players, if you know that one player tells horror stories, another bursts into song while making faces, another explains black holes in the universe, ask them to tell the group! Rather than coaxing great performances from unknowns, make room in your scenario for skills you can count on—like a Singing Dentist, or a Sarcastic Car Washer.

Coach, some participants probably know other participants as well or better than you do; so ask for their help in casting.

You'll see whether or not the right decisions were made as soon as players warm up in character. If you see someone can't do a part, make a switch right away. This is what you might notice:

- A man playing a police captain is soft and lacks leadership.
- A 15-year-old "whiz kid" doesn't have the confidence she needs to compete.
- A woman cast as therapist is not able to listen.

Ask players without parts to invent Bridge Scenes between main scenes. Each Bridge is a design problem that can take 15 minutes to figure out. Extra players are also needed for Crowds—the Joggers, Bikers, Bird Watchers that create a rich active background for the leading players. Give Bridge and Crowd players special attention so they don't feel overlooked.

To make a 30-minute piece you need a lot of bodies—not only to take roles but also to give off energy. A dozen people working alone don't come up with much in the way of ideas, stories, scenes... But put them together. Even the ones who just stand there and nod give strength to the project.

—Elisa Abatsis, Coach

√ Coach's checklist for casting

- Do players accept your coaching? For instance, can they raise their volume, play a game, get into an activity?

- Do they come up with an emotion when you ask for it?

- How far can they play up or down in age?

- Do they talk over each other, or do they listen?

- If players are tense, with arms crossed and face scowling, can you get them to loosen up, touch each other & laugh?
- Do they understand they are *not* being judged? They're being fitted for a part.
- Are they willing not to memorize lines; but let each ending be as much a surprise to themselves as it will be to the viewer?

Shorties

Here's a game to activate players quickly and see how flexible they are. Make a deck of 3x5 cards. On each card, sketch an encounter between two conventional characters. For instance:

- tourist who speaks no English asks directions of local residents who also speak no English.
- coughing nonsmoker begs chain smoker to put out his cigarette.
- laid-back student explains to uptight teacher why he's late.

Players pair up. Each pair chooses one card, then plays out the situation in about a minute. Invent the cards for this group—easy, well-known, classic situations. You don't have to be a pro to play because you know the body language, the hand movements, what words to stress, where the pauses come. You may even have lived through the situation yourself, e.g., stern state trooper & hippie girl driver.

 Testing your characters

Use the camcorder to show players, "This is how you look on tape." Test their belief in their role by shooting them doing a short monolog in character. Replay it.

Figure 11. Evan Shepherd interviews skateboarders for "Bars & Keys" (1985).

Evan Shepherd's Top 5 Tips for Movie Improvs

1) Keep scenes brief and to the point.

2) Mix close-ups and extreme long shots; get close-ups by getting close, not by zooming.

3) Use dramatic locations; thunderstorm, waterfall, Times Square, on a boat, a bonfire, a snowstorm, etc.

4) Ask those off camera to provide organic sound effects such as shouting, humming, tapping, clapping.

5) Find people to play instruments for the intro, outro.

Keep on schedule. Build a sense that the movie is being made not by Project Manager, Camera Operator, Experience Host, or Coach but by the group itself.

5 Warming Up for a Shoot

In most improv troupes, warm-ups are done before the session and then put aside—as if a player who's warmed up will stay warmed up all day! But you can get tense *during* a session. Any time you're not on camera is a good time to warm up.

Of course: the only person who knows you *need* to warm up is you. So ask yourself:

- Am I asleep on my feet, uptight?
- Is something distracting me—in my body, in my mind?
- Are my responses sharp as they could be?
- Am I getting a bit bored?
- Isn't there somebody here I should get to enjoy?
- How about having some fun, folks?
- Tell me, is this fly swatter the right prop for my character?
- Exactly how would my character go about swatting a fly, anyway?

Games

Now make up a collection of the games that work best for you. Mix them up.

- physical
- verbal
- emotional
- rhythmic humming
- throwing things around
- musical

Ask friends to contribute a game.

Invent games while driving, after supper, on the beach...

Are your favorites used? Try some of them now. If you play them well, if you play them hard, your group will grow.

The best reason to warm up is to practice the character you're going to play while getting to know another player.

Pick someone you've improvised with or want to play with and ask, "How about warming up our characters for a few minutes?"

If you both need exercise, just run or walk around briskly—in character. Let your conversation find its own shape. Go with your instincts; you can always pop out of character when you need to. For instance, say, "I'm pulling out now." And when you want to continue, "I'm going back in now."

To sharpen your focus, find an activity that brings you together such as a pack of cards, a newspaper, a crossword puzzle. Activity can sharpen your character as well. How badly do you want to win at cards or show off your knowledge of headlines or find the missing word?

Don't plunge into conflict. Work for agreement. Use the Coach's Signals (5-Second Delay, Contact, Slo/Mo-Fast/Mo, Overlap). Make up your own way to explore character.

≡▶◀ Shooting warm-ups

A warm-up is a good time to show a novice how to shoot because players are now throwing away inhibition and following their intuition. Show the new Camcorder Operator how to use the PAUSE mode to track movement, then RECORD, locking onto the bodies of the players.

At the screening, novices will be glad if a few seconds of their footage on the documentation tape (tape #2) is shown before the story tape.

Freeze Tag

Freeze Tag is today the most popular warm-up for 5 to 10 players. Two players are given characters and a Where. With or without words they launch into their improv as if it will never end. But it is cut—by someone willing to shout, "Freeze!" jump in, and touch one of the players. That player leaves the playing area as the newcomer takes his or her exact position and posture.

The improv continues, but the activity must transform. For instance, say the first pair shoot pool; the second pair find their pool sticks growing into nets on poles. The pool table becomes a tank of piranhas which turn into Kalashnikov rifles in Afghanistan.

Don't make up your mind in advance about what you're going to be or do; *discover it* together with your partner.

Small-of-the-Back Tag

For 6 to 12 players, this game by Keith Johnstone is extremely active; don't play near metal columns or delicate furniture in case players slip. Tag other players as many times as you can on the small of the back or lower down—depending on what country you're in. Don't place your body against a wall where your back can't be touched.

Each touch counts for one point. Tag the small of as many backs as you can touch as many times as you can, shouting out your points as you play— up to 10 or 20. Unless you're playing in a meat freezer, in a few minutes you'll all be sweating.

Run Around the Block

Or stay where you are and do pushups, sit-ups, jump-ups. Exercise lungs & limbs. Sweat. Get loose; breathe deeply.

Figure 12. Some players loosening up their story-telling skills by dancing in Washington Square Park demonstration (1995). Photo credit: Author.

Yes!!!

Yes!!! by Izzy Gesell is for a group of any size. Players stroll around aimlessly. The Leader then uses a loud, enthusiastic voice to introduce a physical activity, for example, "Let's go skydiving."

Everybody responds by shouting, "Yes!!!" then dives through the sky until someone suggests a second activity.

For example, "Let's drink tea and eat crumpets."

"Yes!!!" the group responds and then pantomimes drinking tea and eating tiny sandwiches.

Figure 13. Izzy Gesell.
Photo credit: Author

Your Week That Was

For Your Week That Was by Michael Golding, stand in a circle. One after another *describe in words* the day you just lived through. Take less than a minute to do it. Then repeat the whole memory—communicating this time nonverbally.

Merge

A player starts an activity—such as a monk weeding a garden. Observers ask questions of the monk, who responds in character. Then a second player in a different character joins the first; together they continue the activity, which transforms as they talk. The first player finds an excuse to leave. The audience asks questions of this new player, who continues the new activity while answering. Soon a third player approaches....

Figure 14. Canadian and American Coaches warm up for "Sound & Motion."

Character Relay

Character Relay is from the ImprovOlympix. Pick two players who are of different genders or *clearly have real differences* (in personality, speech, attitude). They ask observers where to be and what characters to play. They pick up simple props. After a minute or two of improvisation, a Coach says, "Freeze. Exchange props. Switch positions. Switch characters." The improv continues for another minute or two. At a second signal the players switch back and find an ending for the improv.

Talking Ball

Three or more players stand in a circle with a small ball. A player says a word while tossing the ball to another player. That player immediately says the first word that comes to mind while tossing the ball to a third player. Anyone who pauses or repeats a word is out.

⌘ Collect games

Like jokes, warm-ups are being invented as we speak. So keep your ears and eyes open for new ones. Invent your own. And use them freely *during the shoot* as well as before.

Raw Improv

The most exciting scene I remember was played in Chicago by nonprofessionals: a Polish cook and his waiter, about 10 a.m. in a restaurant.

The cook was cleaning his stove while the waiter put out napkins and silverware. I don't understand Polish, but their interaction was intense, bitter, loud, responsive, full of movement. At the height of rage, the scene had intimacy.

The players were totally at home in this location. They didn't try to shape their emotion because each emotion took its own shape. No flourishes or pauses had to be invented. They didn't try to give the scene a point because their raw emotions were the point.

6 Bringing Improv to Video

Over-the-Shoulder Voice-Overs

Two players start a silent activity that can be shot in one area, such as:

- folding laundry
- sweeping and dusting
- painting a surface
- waxing a car

The third player shoots—moving so the two subjects are always in the frame. The camera catches one player full face and the other on the side of the face. This called shooting over the shoulder

The fourth player provides a voice-over (improvised song, monolog for one of the players, news, sound effect).

On playback, see how the voice-over meshes with the activity or contrasts it.

I'm not an actor, but Paul Sills asked me to play the Minister in a scenario at COMPASS cabaret. Every time I opened my mouth, self-contempt rolled out. So Paul gave me to Elaine May for a tune-up. She asked, "Who are you doing, David?"

I said, "I'm doing this guy I heard at Union Theological Seminary."

"Try playing your father." She sat there waiting for me to climb into my Daddy's persona.

I said to myself, "The Minister is not my father. The Minister is phony, and my father is true-blue. So this characterization is false." But I did what Elaine said.

Normally we want people to like us, and we cover up reasons to think badly of ourselves. But I was begging the audience to *dislike* me—both for the way I treated my kids, and for my spaced-out politics. But after my tune-up, every time I lost my self-respect on stage, the image of my father would drag me back to it.

For instance, if a hippie friend (Haym Berenson) of my daughter (Barbara Harris) put his face into my face and said, "Father, why is your tie so long?" I'd pop back into being *my* father. No matter how cold and pretentious my character, I now wanted the audience to like me. To play my father I didn't have to study his character; I knew it cold from 35 years of observation.

Going on camera is like going on stage. Some participants shy away from play in MOVIExperience. They regard the professional actor as slick and confident, and they see themselves as the opposite. "I stutter," they protest. "I'm too short; I'm too tall; I won't know what to say."

At Chicago City Limits, a school in New York City, students learn that the minute you step on stage, whether you are professional or amateur, you lose half your intelligence. Your attention is drawn away from what you're doing to who's out there in the dark observing how you look and what you say.

So this fear is perfectly normal, and there are three simple ways to overcome it:

- focus
- feeling
- character

Focus on Activity

Off camera we drink coffee while reading the paper, shine our shoes while talking on the phone. That's to say, we have a point of concentration; we're in focus. All our attention has been sucked into activities. Our mouths and ears and fingers are all busy. We don't have time to be anxious.

Waiting to go on camera we have little to do. So we're aware of lights, camera, Coach, technicians, and even people who may see us on the tape in the future. As we get uptight, it's natural that the mind clutches, feelings freeze, and we make mistakes.

The job of your Coach is to make you as comfortable in a spotlight as you are in your armchair at home. One way to do this is by helping you focus.

We can focus on points *external* to our body:

- our hands washing a stack of dishes
- our eyes watching a chickadee at the feeder
- our ears listening to sports news on the radio

√ Using props for focus

These *pocket props* trigger activities that give you focus: fingernail clipper, comb, brush, keys, newspaper. Name three more you would use.

_____

Here are some *table props* to bring to a shoot: dice, cards, calculator, bud vase, invitation, photo. Name three more.

_____

Find larger *props on location* that can be used: computer, microwave, rake, vacuum cleaner, giant cactus. Name three more.

_____

Then there are *internal* points, for example:

- our nerves telling us we have an ache in the left shoulder
- our memory gloating over a winning bet at the race track

⌘ Find activities for yourself in these locations

- stalled elevator at midnight

  _____

- street corner at 4 p.m.

  _____

- empty barn at dawn

  _____

- 20th floor motel room at 6 p.m.

  _____

- art gallery on Sunday afternoon

  _____

- mountain top at sunset

  _____

- office lobby at 8 a.m. waiting for an interview

  _____

One of the easiest points to focus on is your costume. Have you noticed how much people are adjusting their clothes and their hair?

Focus on Feeling

A player who's angry or delighted or filled with love automatically has confidence in what she or he is doing. A feeling is driving the player; it justifies whatever happens. And if all players on camera have a strong feeling, much more will happen in the improv than if they don't.

How can you load real feeling onto your character? Here are two ways to bring out whatever you feel at any time, so you can use it in the improv:

Mood Swing

In this Coach's Signal, you choose your own starting emotion, then swing to the extreme opposite emotion. For example, swing from expressing anger to delight or from fear to pride. (Also discussed in Chapter 7.)

Talk, Answer, Respond

Jonathon Appel calls this an organic approach since it brings out whatever feeling you already have in you.

Standing close together, you talk, your partner answers, then you respond as strongly as you can, for example:

You talk: "I see where it's going to snow 6 inches."

Your partner answers: "I don't care."

You respond: "You don't care? You might be out there with a stalled car, sloshing around in six inches of muck, with ice slicing into your toes and you don't care? What's the matter with you?"

Now you've discovered how you feel.

Figure 15. Ken Coleman and David Lutzer. two strangers, demonstrate Contact in Washington Square Park. Photo credit: Author

Body Feeling

Players find their own feeling by letting it out through their bodies: they swing their arms, stamp, snap their fingers, jump, roll on the ground, shiver, twirl, spin, shake...

Best & Worst

Still another organic way: close your eyes and think about the best & worst moments of your life. Choose the first that comes up—or the strongest—and use that emotion in the scene. Seize other times of your life when you felt great pride, panic, boredom, ecstasy, disgust, lust, anger (these are all primal emotions).

⌘ Play Best & Worst

Recall the worst moment of your life.

Stay there until you grasp the full feeling again.

Recall the best moment of your life.

Stay there; remember your environment; who was there with you; what they did.

Grab Bag

Fill a bag with slips of paper marked with emotions, for instance: *argue—lament—console—boast—laugh.* Ask each player to pull out a slip on the way to the camera.

There's nothing like being out there on the town making up stories and enacting them, moving spontaneously, and letting the camera capture our fantasy, our realism, or the life of our group.

All is possible. The shy lose their shyness; the outgoing discover deeper layers of relationship; the lawyer acts out his argument; the professional actor gains a freer and more spontaneous path.

David Haber,
Professor Emeritus of Law,
Rutgers Law School, NJ.

Yourself as Character

Many professional actors find the amateur boring. Of course if a female accountant, let's say, is given the role of police chief or belly dancer, her performance may be boring or even embarrassing. But if the same player plays *herself,* frantically finishing returns on April 15, or advising a client about going bankrupt, then she's at home. We have the pleasure of seeing her little-known life open up. Could professionals open it better? Although they can shape scenes and produce feeling, they probably know little about accounting.

Let's say you turn down the roles of belly dancer & police chief, but they need you for nurse or CEO. You know nothing about these professions. That's all right; you can still look good on camera.

Choose a powerful feeling—*disgust,* for instance. As the nurse, enter the improv with authority, then find the location and what happens there, *disgusting.* Or as the CEO, play *fatigue.* You have such severe jet lag you barely respond to the day's problems.

On top of having a physical condition and feeling, assume that this is your first day on the job: you have a poor grasp of procedures. And don't be embarrassed by your lack of expertise. If anything, be louder and more demanding than others beside you who have worked here for years.

Character Exercises

Plastic People from Grotowski

For a group of a half dozen, in silence make believe you are all made of a plastic that's slowly melting and reshaping itself. At a cue, freeze! You each see what shape you've taken. Hold it. Now choose a way to talk to each other as if you are all in the same family, party, or work force. At another cue, melt and move again. Do this about three times—or until you've found a body shape that suggests a character you can play.

Behavior Plus Feeling

Choose a behavior very different from your own (for example, talking nonstop, knocking objects around). Choose a feeling to complement or contrast that behavior (for instance, showing off, complaining about the way you're treated). Practice mixing these two qualities until you have a character that you can use on camera.

In building a character, start inside and work out: how does the character breathe, stand, walk? How do the arms move, the hands, the head? Where's the center of gravity —in belly, thighs, forehead?

Figure 16. Melinda Nielsen plays a holistic aunt at Nancy Fletcher's suggestion. A core character for "Family Reunion" (2001), our first Team Play Mode. Photo credit: Nikhil Melnechuck.

Impersonate Someone You Know Well

There are probably a half-dozen close friends and family members whom you can impersonate outrageously. Do one now, fast. Keep it in mind for the farmer, taxi driver, or hacker you may be given to play.

Monolog

Look into a mirror, or out the window, and express your gut feelings—in character or as yourself. At the Brainstorm offer a monolog. It may fit perfectly between two scenes.

Three Through the Door

Your partner establishes a location with a door as entrance. You come through the door in character and improvise with him or her for 2 to 3 minutes. Find a reason to exit, and return as a totally different character. Do this 3 times. Then switch roles with your partner.

Building Familiarity on Camera

How to build familiar relationships between people who don't know each other? One way is to imagine you have X-ray vision; other players appear naked to you! Here's another:

Let's say you're playing strangers on a subway platform at midnight. In real life you'd probably keep your distance and say nothing. But for the scene to be interesting, some feeling must emerge. Try this: the woman treats the stranger like Ivan, the body builder she jokes with at her health club. The man assumes the strange woman is lost because she reminds him of Lulu, his little lost sister.

This scene, between a powerful Ivan and a vulnerable Lulu, is now dynamic, charged. Instead of dying in silence and suspicion, the improv will move on the assumption that something will happen between these two.

Suppose you're doing a scene about a husband & wife doing dishes. Instantly you must feel married! But how? Try this—both of you take on a strong attitude:

The husband assumes she's super finicky and much older.

She assumes he'll break a glass—because he's a clumsy child.

Now you have a relationship on which an improv can grow.

Intimacy

A small group stands in a circle. Each player reveals who the other players remind him of, then follows up with a personal comment, for instance:

"You remind me of my grandma; what's that spot on your cheek?"

"You remind me of my daughter; that's a funny outfit you chose to wear today."

"You look like my old girlfriend Christine; I love the way your hair swishes around your head."

Next: pair up. Choose a location and discover how you relate by doing a short improv.

Four Fun Ways to Familiarity

Here are some other games to help you build familiarity.

Gibberish Switch

Choose a topic to talk about in English, giving and taking clearly. At signals from the Coach, switch instantly to Gibberish then back to English, then back to Gibberish—keeping the same topic. The Coach will interrupt you in the middle of your sentence, so be prepared to switch instantly.

Wing It

Taking turns, guess the color of your partner's underwear, favorite game, candy, food, music, actor, actress, deepest fear or greatest desire. Then share the reality.

Birthday Overlap

Talking together, each player describe his/her last birthday. Then take turns: tell your partner how much of his/her birthday description you can remember and vice versa.

Totally True

Tell a story that's either a total invention or totally true. Your partner guesses which it is, then tells his own story. You guess. Share the reality. Before you begin agree on how long stories will be.

 Shoot Doubling

Use props, costume pieces, accent, posture to see how many different characters you can come up with.

Look for a body language for each character. The camera operator frames your head, RECORDS and CUTS as you change character, then RECORDS again.

Want to know how convincing you are? Check yourself out on video monitor. What you'll see is a series of precise cameos in which your skull is motionless while your characters go through changes.

Improv Dos and Don'ts

- Don't deny your partner

If your partner says, "Let's play Ping-Pong," don't respond with "No, thanks" or with silence. Keep the creativity flowing by building on your partner's responses, not tearing them down or ignoring them.

- Stay in the Here & Now.

Not the There & Then. Instead of telling us about your grandfather in World War II, tell us about your own patriotism today.

- Instead of questions, use statements.

"You're cold! Let me wrap you up" moves the scene forward. "Are you cold? Would you like me to wrap you up?" slows the scene down.

- Don't try to control the scene by using irrelevant material.

"By the way, I won the Lottery," takes the scene to where you alone can control it. "Loan me $10 till Tuesday" brings the scene back to your partner.

- Stay in focus while playing.

Focus on your activity, physical irritation, temperature, weather, or the environment (for example, birds feeding, a distant siren, smell of wood burning, the feeling your partner is hiding).

- Commit to the scene.

If the scene is about firing a worker, don't make an abrupt phone call to your sister-in-law. Stay on the point. Trust yourselves to work it through to the end.

- Give & take.

Listen to your partner just as you do in real life. Don't let the camera throw you into a frenzy of what is called steamrolling, in which you dominate by talking loudly and pushing your partner around.

- Your costume

The easiest way to improve a video: all players wear a costume piece. No one goes on camera unless there is something on the head, chest, hands, legs...Most of the costume pieces you need can be found in your closet. It's precisely old stuff that's about to be thrown out (boa or sombrero) that can make your character vivid on video. A costume piece helps the viewer identify who is who—scene to scene.

- Props

Find the prop that brings out your character, and get used to using it so it looks natural on camera. Props like a still camera, cell phone, bubblegum or cigar provide you with a natural activity. Put unique props in your pockets: an antique coin, for instance, matchbox from a bar, unfamiliar key. Take them out one at a time. See what character each suggests to you.

*In my experience amateurs can be awful while some are ex-
cellent. I've also learned that professionals can be excellent
while many are awful.*

—Michael Golding
Trainer and screenwriter

√ Player's checklist to get ready for a shoot

■ **basic choice**—Am I going to play the scene as myself or as a character?

■ **as myself**—How am I dressed? How do I want to be seen?

■ **focus**—What internal irritation am I aware of (a runny nose, ringing in
my ears, an itch behind my shoulder)? What external focus (ap-
proaching storm, distant crow, smell of perfume)?

■ **relaxation**—Am I tight or loose physically? How fast does my breath
come, how deep?

■ **feelings**—How do I feel today about myself, about others?

■ **costume**—What costume piece (helmet, fur coat, granny glasses) can
make my role instantly clear? What prop can enrich my character?

■ **consciousness**—What's on my mind most of the time (social position,
romance, sports, debts, health, Internet)?

■ **body**—What's my weight, posture, stride, arm position, hand movements? What do my fingers do? How does my head connect to my
neck?

■ **speech**—How do I sound different from others like me—in volume,
pace, accent?

Having a MOVIExperience

Making a movie cassette is straight forward; just follow the steps
of this guide. But how do you capture the experience part or the
magical interactions that weave together during production? In 1994
it was this for me:

Buffet breakfast in NYC, makeup, learning lines, rehearsal, the
shoot, watching equipment in action, schmoozing off-camera, seeing
myself on tape, continuity photos in my mail, a party thrown by Rich-
mond, the producer.

His cassette, "Gurney Man," was not distributed, but the "experience" of making it was for me indelible. It propelled me to carry
scenarios and equipment to many states, sharing with hundreds of
people that first delicious taste.

If you get a couple dozen people to pay full attention to each other, hammer out their story together, and bring it to life, you're going to precipitate dozens of experiences like these:

Seven of you lose vote #1 at the Brainstorm, but your scenario wins on vote #2!... sound effects are needed, and you promptly create them on a boombox...players slink about—muttering monologs for characters they plan to play...from screen tests you figure out which player to cast as the heavy.

In the afternoon a bunch of you watch rushes from the morning shoot... there's this non-stop, all-day argument going on about the latest Brad Pitt movie...scuttlebutt is thick about local jobs in film production and broadcast...your opinion is accepted by the Camcorder Operator shooting the poker scene.

You do the makeup for the fat guy who's been cast as a con man...the croupier seeks your opinion about how to rake in the money...a Portuguese woman asks if her German accent is too fake...you munch on cheddar Goldfish crackers while predicting who'll be in next year's movie.

A glamorous player on the set warms up with you, shares a secret ambition...six of you look over an hour of rushes and pick scenes to edit into a movie for cable...there's a goof in continuity! You tell the Coach; it gets fixed... the CD you bring, with a song on it for the movie, is heard and used.

You're asked if the baseball hat a player wears should be pink or orange...goofing on Santa Claus, your rap proves to be perfect for Scene 8...you steady the Camcorder Operator by holding her belt when she shoots down off a table...you help a player master the sea-legs swagger of a Gloucester fisherman.

You help coach the ditsy redhead to make her betrayal scene believable...Take II of your Police Chief is the strongest piece in the movie...you get the feel for throwing light on faces at a dusky poker scene...to get perfect sound you learn where to pin the lavaliere mic.

You hold the boom mic on a group without once letting it peek into the frame...quickly you rearrange props so a scene's point is made nonverbally...a player uses your joke about the antiques business so she looks like a real dealer... two of you do big calisthenics before your scene so you're well grounded.

You show the Project Manager where continuity's broken down again... having so many opinions about costumes, you're given the Costume job!...you're recruited for a crowd scene where you'll be visible waist down only.

You find a way to play a second role in the bar scene without being recognized...a Bridge that fits nicely between scenes is invented by you...you turn a weak scene inside out—to make it work in the scenario...it turns out a cool couple you meet lives only a half-mile from you.

You unwrap your pot at the pot luck supper and savor what others have cooked.

As our format develops through the Twenty-first Century, alongside other formats we have yet to discover, there are plenty of other experiences people will have.

7 Coach and Play the Games

Can Improv Be Directed?

Take turns—everyone on staff pretending to be a coach. While 2 or more players play, you direct them, for instance, to:

- speak louder or softer
- experience a dominant emotion such as grief, joy, suspicion
- be agitated, calm while reading a newspaper
- repeat a line from a song
- do a movement in a different way, like tipping the bartender

Test the limits of your power to direct improv.

You may never again have such willing subjects.

What's the difference between a theatre Director & an improv Coach? The Director thinks of an actor as a very interesting lump of clay, to be carefully molded and shaped. The improv Coach treats a player like an energy that's been donated to the movie. It can't be changed but can be guided.

The Director can't change the scene while it's in progress.

The Coach *can* use sound cues to coach the scene while it's happening. A tapping noise will not be noticed on the sound track, but will signal players to stop (or start) using a game. A Coach works with what's already there, asking

- with this cast and scenario, what can be done in this location?
- can this uptight customer be warmed up so she plays the kittenish baby sitter?
- what game will give life to this boring moment?
- since Take I is shaky, should we delete it and shoot Take II?
- for Take II, what new game will give fresh energy to the improv?

When working with a small group, a Coach can take the job of Project Manager, too.

The Coach looks out for bad acting, which can pop up at any time—for instance, if players chatter and refuse to allow anything to happen.

√ How to tell good improv acting from...bad

Strong improv	Weak improv
You believe it.	You definitely don't believe it
Do they listen to each other?	Do they talk over each other?
Do they build on what each other offers?	Do they deny each other?
Are *bad* characters believable?	Do *good* characters turn you off?
Are emotions right for the given situation?	Are emotions used for effect—to show off?
Do players use a variety of expressions?	Do players hang onto one tone or feeling?
Do they stay in the here and now?	Do they overplay to make a point because they don't trust you to get it?
Are they committed; do they follow actions through?	Are they so distracted they don't finish what they start?
other:_____	_____

Talk about it. Which kinds of acting do you want to cut out of your movie? A word from some coaches:

"With one of us around, you look good on camera. We make sure you're wearing a hat, dark glasses, a rose, or some other costume piece. We give you a newspaper, a nail file, or some other prop to focus on. We get you into warm-ups, and the warm-ups get you into your role.

"When a scene misses the point or is unbelievable, inaudible, badly framed... then we stop it. We ask the Camera Operator to rewind tape so we can shoot it again."

Jasper, Barbara, Michael, Howard, David, Al, Izzy, Philip, Ellen, Marybeth, Andrea, John, Nancy, Elisa

---

⌘ **Play Cut It Out**

Pair off. Each pair choose an example of bad acting—exaggerated, talkative, emotionally fake, etc. One after another each pair gets up and demonstrates their kind of bad acting. When the ones who are watching guess *how* the acting is bad, the improv ends.

Coach's Signals

The Coach suggests one of these games before an improv begins. The cast uses that game for warm-up. Whenever the scene is paused for a moment, a different Signal can be introduced, or the Signal can be removed if the improv is hot.

5-Second Delay

Talk less and open the scene to feeling. Use short responses only—with 5 seconds of silence between responses. Justify the delay; there must be some reason for it. (The Coach can also ask for a 3-second delay, for instance, or 10-second delay.) Camera, move in close to catch reaction shots.

Figure 17. On the left Jr. is playing tough guy in silence while Cordero can't believe what he sees. Photo: Hronn Axelsdottir.

Sample patter for the Coach. "This Game is about justifying a short silence. Make it look natural to *feel* something, rather than flip off a snappy response. Use short sentences. While we're learning, I'm going to count 1..., 2..., 3..., 4..., 5. So don't speak until you hear 5,

OK? Rob and Ray, you now are brothers at the casket of your class-mate—a woman.

ROB: Wow.

COACH: 1..., 2..., 3..., 4..., 5.

RAY: Why did this have to happen to *her*?

COACH: 1..., 2..., 3..., 4..., 5.

ROB: Always had bad luck.

COACH: Good. Now count for yourselves—silently.

RAY: The worst. [Grips Rob's shoulder, counting silently.]

COACH: Rob, you're just freezing and counting. Give yourself a sigh or a sniffle or whatever makes the silence real.

Contact

Translate your relationship into the physical—a game of Viola Spolin. If you want to talk, you must touch your partner. If you want to talk again, touch your partner a different way.

Sample side coaching for Contact: "Never touch the same way twice. Show how you feel about each other. How do you feel about yourself? Are you pushy, coy, assertive, flamboyant? Hey Pete, you touched her already on the left shoulder. Linda, you shook hands once already. Find something else. Don't forget each other's backs. Don't forget knees, ears lobes...."

Figure 18. Coach's Signal, Contact (2003). Photo credit: Chester Cramer.

Slo/Mo

At a Slo/Mo signal, players move slower and talk slower (but at the same pitch as before). Slo/Mo slows down what's happening in a scene—use it with a strong activity. Make the change look natural. You're tired, for instance, it's hot, or you've been drinking beer.

Sample patter for coach: "Try a game that cuts down on wordiness and gets up some feeling: Slo/Mo. When I give you a signal, move slower and talk slower. Stick pauses into everything you do. Ready? 1...2...3.... Marge, you're still talking too fast. S l o w! Henry, you can *move* slower, can't you? Good..."

Fast/Mo

Fast/Mo builds energy and trust between players. Speed up your movements & talk faster without changing pitch. Make the change look natural by showing danger, excitement, time-pressure.

Sample patter: "This is Fast/Mo. Find a reason for moving and talking faster. You've got to catch a train. Or it's 50 degrees below. All right, see if you can do everything at twice your normal speed. You're making sandwiches, OK? Try it....Gladys, why are *you* moving so fast?"

"I've got to go to the bathroom."

"Good. Do you all know *why* you're so speedy? Now bring it back to Normal Mo...."

Mood Swing

Players practice going from one full emotion to another. Give two players a location; give each a primal emotion—like love, fear, hate, boredom, lust, disgust, enjoyment, pride, anger... During the game each player finds a second primal emotion to play.

Sample patter: "Leonard, I don't get what you're feeling. Show it to us in your body. Clara, that's very clear. Now start switching into a second emotion that's rising inside you."

Figure 19. Coach's Signal, Mood Swing. Photo credit: Claudia Gere

In the field, ask the players to warm up for the game by playing their two emotions nonverbally but fully. Don't shoot the scene until you're sure players have reached the top of their feelings.

Overlap

To boost energy, two or more players talk at the same time. Because one shouts in bursts and the other whispers, because one talks rapidly and the other slowly, because one talks at a high pitch and the other at a low pitch, both can be understood!

Sample patter: "Here's a game for instant energy. You talk at the same time as your partner(s). First get into some activity: you're at a barbeque cooking ribs. 1, 2, 3, go.... George, you stopped! Find an excuse to keep on talking. Good. Now lower your voice way down and talk a little slower. Gladys, raise your voice and speak rapidly. Listen to that: I understand you both! That's called Overlap."

"Let's try one more thing: when I stand up, do Overlap. When I sit down, go back to normal. OK: the way I'll signal you is by standing up or sitting. See me out of the corner of your eye. Don't look at me, please, or you ruin the shot."

Nonverbal

Continue a relationship but without words. Players put energy into activities and into grunts, whistling, singing, hitting things....

Sample patter: "Ever been in a situation where you wouldn't talk or you couldn't talk? Like in a library or at a final exam? Well, give us a situation like that—somebody...a sick room? OK. Who's playing the patient?...Sit here. And the nurse?...Fine. The doctor?...Let's go. You can make noises, but *no words*. Bertrand, is that sign language you're using? Please don't attempt to communicate by wiggling your fingers and blinking your eyes. This exercise is about feeling, not communication."

Three Words

In Three Words by Keith Johnstone, you must respond to the person who speaks before you using 3 words. If you use 2 words, you're out. If you respond using 4 words, you're out.

Status Switch

This game by Keith Johnstone for two players guarantees something happens besides talk. One plays a person of authority and confidence, the other a person who has no power and little self-esteem.

As the scene progresses, they change their feeling about themselves: the person of high status becomes low and vice versa.

Figure 20. Coach's Signal, Status Switch, changing authority.

Close/Far

Find out if you're seen & heard. Create a relationship about three feet from the camera mic, using limited movement and whispering. Gradually move away, raising your volume and expanding your gestures. Then play back the tape to see if you can be heard—and seen—from beginning to end. New players almost never talk loud enough. I tell them that I'm hard of hearing or that they're talking against a gale.

The Be Game

We found it was impossible to Be Boring. The further you went into the routine of boredom, the funnier it got. Today we signal whoever is on camera to Be Boring. Or Be Disgusted. Or Be Delighted. Make up your own.

Figure 21. Coach's Signal, The Be Game, being stuck up.

=︎🦗   **Participants shoot**

Here's your chance to let participants shoot—a big part of the Experience of making a video movie. First shoot a scene with no Coach's Signal, then with one. Play the tape back and compare.

Checklist for Coaching Basics

- Make players feel you're confident about the shoot
- Grasp the physical & emotional range of each player
- Pick Signals likely to make players comfortable & expressive
- Predict when a scene is going to fail; stop it before it crashes by saying, "Cut! Let's do Take II."
- Don't move to the next location unless something real has happened between players, and it's on the tape.

What will happen? What most improvs do (just as in real life encounters) is move the players forward on the track of *their relationship*. We want to see not a dead end but change. As Coach you can make change likely.

Before you shoot:

- remind players where the story is, where it could go and how it could get there
- do players have feelings, attitudes, goals? Get some.
- are they in focus? Are they in the here and now?

Them–Us

Choose a location. Every player plays the character farthest away from him and at a signal plays himself again. For instance, players all play their parents, then themselves, then their kids (or kids they could have), then themselves, then an animal that's like their character...then a hijacker...a mayor....

Feeling Is a Must

Players who have feeling are more open to a change of relationship than players who don't. And change of relationship is what any good scene is about. For instance: a mother gets furious with her daughter's sloppiness, then realizes her own room is sloppy too, then apologizes, then helps her daughter clean up, then laughs with relief, then gets stern—while the daughter goes through many feelings, too.

Make sure players coming on camera are brimming over with feeling. Here are some ways to do that:

- play Mood Swing (Coach's signal); you give the starting emotion
- make a grab bag in which you put slips of paper marked with feelings; each player picks one up on the way to the camera

Asking for Feedback

Letting everyone know that you're tuned in to their experience is important.

⌘ —Sample feedback questions

In this workshop a Coach will ask you for feedback.

Are you hot, cold, comfortable? _____

Does the person speaking make sense? _____

Is it boring? _____

Is it going too fast, too slow? _____

Are you learning what you want to learn? _____

Are you enjoying yourself? _____

Do you want more written material—about what? _____

_____

Do you want to work on our next movie?_____

Changing Improv Elements

Imagine you're shooting a scene in which a couple decides at 2 a.m. who's going to stay up with their sick baby. Here are elements for an improv; you can change all of them.

⌘ What a Coach can change	
scenario	Is the scene clear? What's the relationship of the man and woman? What could happen? What must happen—according to the scenario? Does the scenario require a certain ending?
location	How could the location be changed so the improv gets richer, funnier, more ironic, or colorful? How long would it take to make the change?
characters	Are they believable, consistent, interesting? If not, is it too late to make a cast change? Would the players object?
props/costumes	What's available? What has each player chosen? Does it work?
activity	Will it be a toothpick, mosquito, or newscast that gives the player focus?
feeling	Are players available to feeling? Are they ready to express it?
lighting	Should the Camera Operator move it, amplify it, reduce it?
sound	Has the Camera Operator checked for the noise of an air conditioner or fan? Does the scene need a boombox radio or music? Who will make the sound of the sick baby, of the party going on up stairs?
Coach's Signal	Do you need one? Have players do it before the shoot. How will you remove it once it's done what you want, or if it *doesn't* do what you want.

If you have strong players, most of these elements fall right into place. The element I forget is hats. Your movie is always better if players remember a hat, toothpick, a wet bandana, and other reminders of who they are.

Bottom line: after every take, scan the video. Make sure the image is clean and the sound clear—before going on to the next take.

8 Camcorder Operator Basics

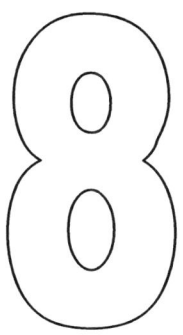

Glitchery

A glitch occurs at the end of a take where the picture loses its stability for several frames.

Using an old cassette, find a spot on the tape where one scene ends and another starts. Now, shoot a new take.

See if your new take is a clean in-camera edit. Then rewind or fast forward the camcorder before passing it to another member of your group.

Everyone gets practice making a clean in-camera edit without recording over the last scene or leaving a glitch.

This chapter takes you, hands-on, into the use of your equipment.

A Camcorder is not a still camera that squeezes the heads, feet, hands, and home of your subjects into one snapshot for the scrapbook.

It's not a device that frames a face and waits for spotlights to be adjusted so a perfect portrait is achieved.

A camcorder zooms right into your face—to pick up feeling, which can be read only by studying eyes, wrinkles, eyebrows, mouth. *It frames action by moving around the subjects*, who are themselves in motion.

If the subject runs, the Camcorder can't say, "Hold up so I can take your picture." The Camcorder runs, too. If the light is bad, the Camcorder does its best by raising gain (adjusting aperture), zooming in on a part of the body that's in light, or backing off to get a silhouette.

Think of your Camcorder as an extra player who sees things differently. Now it shoots from the pavement to record heels. Now it's on the ceiling to catch a poker game below. Now it moves back 100 yards from the lovers because it wants them bathed in foliage. It sits inside the refrigerator to see light crack wide as the door swings open.

Use Macro

If you don't know how to adjust your focus to macro (extreme close-up), then read your camcorder manual. Macro brings a usually unseen world into focus. You see the conformation of a buttercup, the legs of a spider, the inscription on a silver broach.

Macro shots are short—one or two seconds are plenty. If each of your group members shoots 3 frames, you'll get a tape that runs less than a minute.

When editing, extreme close-ups are useful to sandwich longer material. By adding music you can create what we call default footage, returning again and again to the same compact video signature.

Treat the Scene as a Game

Find a prop that brings out your character and get used to using it so it looks natural on camera. Props such as a still camera, cell phone, bubblegum, or cigar provide you with a natural activity.

Shoot action as if it were a sport. Circle the players, move in for a close-up of a face, move out for a long shot of the group. Plan ahead as little as possible; take your cue from what's happening. When we say a scene has *life*, we're saying it's unpredictable. That's what we want to say about your footage.

Figure 22. If this scene were shot from a low angle, it would make the group look like a crowd. "House of the Dream" (1988). Photo credit: Woody Ford.

Let the Improv Get up to Speed

Instead of giving players on location a countdown, the Coach may say, "Just start the scene." You've covered the red light on the camera so no one can tell if it's recording. When the improv gets interesting; that is, when *something starts to happen* between players, then the Coach taps you on the shoulder—your signal to RECORD.

Editing in Camera

The technical term *editing in camera* means the camera does not shoot take after take, and then go off to a studio for screening to edit out the best footage. It doesn't shoot material before or after the improv. When you edit in camera, you hit RECORD a couple of seconds before the *exact* picture you want, and you hit PAUSE a couple of seconds after the *exact* end you want. Screen your tape to see how it looks and sounds. If you and your Coach don't like a take, REWIND then shoot again.

Cut Down the Talk

Improv can get talky and, on replay, boring. With your Coach's OK, speed it up by making internal cuts.

- At the end of one sentence PAUSE your camcorder.
- Take a new position, frame & focus.
- At the end of another sentence, RECORD again.

This technique can slash verbiage and raise the energy of the scene. Screen your footage to make sure you haven't erased a crucial detail. If you did, reshoot.

Remember, improvs on stage last a couple of minutes, but the average take in a finished film is only a few seconds. By editing in camera, video approaches the pace of film.

Pan and Swish Pan

A *pan* is a shot in which the camera pivots horizontally—slow and steady. A *swish pan* is a fast horizontal shot. Try ending an improv by rapidly moving away from players and to the background behind them. Screen footage in the view finder and stop the camcorder where the swish pan loses interest; that's where you'll start the next scene.

If you want players to be heard *before* they are seen, start your scene with a pan that swings toward them until it frames them.

A pan gives you loose footage between scenes. Good: if you want to shoot Take II, you can start it at just about any point of the pan. A pan also tells the viewer more about where action is taking place.

Tilt

A vertical pan is called a *tilt*. To reveal what's happening, travel from the wet street to an air plane in the sun, for instance, or from white ceiling to dusty shoes. Example: the camera tilts from rain clouds down the facade of an abandoned tenement and comes to rest on a bride holding a bouquet.

Get comfortable shooting

Seat some friends at a table: talking, drinking, reading, playing cards. Ask them not to look at the camera. Tell them that most of them will do the same exercise after you. (Who will be sharp enough to assist on your next short movie?)

The exercise:

Shoot down.	Stand on a sturdy table or ladder. Tilt the camera down to capture all your subjects in a wide shot. Zoom in to frame a torso and head. Notice how much less imposing people appear. Zoom in to frame hands. Pan from one pair of hands to another.
Shoot up.	Put the camcorder on the floor. Ask players for some foot movement. Shoot a dialog of shoes and boots. Now ask your friends to stand. Shoot up at faces. Notice how dominant they now appear.
How close can you get?	Shoot earrings, bracelets, buckles, glasses, and other accoutrements—showing as little flesh as possible. Then shoot flesh—nose, moustache, ear lobe. Use the macro function (see your manual) to do extreme close-ups of the same subjects. How much closer does that take you—to 6 inches, 2 inches?

Choosing Cutaways

A *cutaway* is a well-framed still shot—3 to 5 seconds long—of something in the environment. While shooting your subject, try looking quickly for a cutaway. For instance, tilt down to a person's hands. While shooting the hands, look for another cutaway, such as a sweating glass of cold coke. Go back and forth till you run out of objects that can enrich the subject.

Figure 23. These teddy bears provided just the right cutaway for a love scene.

A cutaway can connect two scenes. Wherever an improv ends is a good place to put a meaningful object on the tape. Would a rose petal be an appropriate cameo for a story about money? No, but a Lotto ticket lying on a pile of change would.

The viewer expects a cutaway to be relevant. It should relate to what's happening in the scene. If the scene is about surgery, for instance, cutaway to a scalpel—not to a fashion magazine. As you pan away rapidly and then back to the operation, your mic continues to pick up dialog. PAUSE, frame the new object, RECORD, PAUSE, reframe the main scene and go on recording.

Getting Rid of Jump Cuts in Edit

If you cut a long interview to a couple of minutes, you'll have *jump cuts*. In this footage the subject seems to jump. Let's say, from the left side of the frame to the right.

If the subject stayed rigidly in the same position for an hour, you'd have *match cuts*. But the subject can't do that, and you wouldn't want it. You want your subject to move freely.

Start your shot by recording things that will not be shot in the interview, for instance:

- the subject's hands in his or her lap, moving
- a glass filled with whatever the subject is drinking
- a newspaper opened to a headline
- on the wall, a photo of the subject taken years before
- a tabletop covered with things important to the subject

When you insert these cutaways, you make the jump cuts vanish. You also provide us with information about the subject that he or she doesn't reveal during the interview. If you forget to shoot cutaways, you won't be able to edit much of your footage.

Bridges

A *bridge* is longer than a cutaway, briefly showing some interaction, movement, or conversation that fits in with scenes before and after it.

You finish shooting Scene 6. You need a 5-minute break to get players ready for Scene 7. Ask some of them to invent a bridge about:

- what happens on sidewalks in this part of town, for instance
- who's trading jokes at the nearest bar
- where the 10-year-old juggler from Scene 1 went to
- why the people in Scene 2 are still arguing
- guy who tries to park a big car in a small space

Here are some sample bridges:

- Two businesswomen with tubes & cases walk through puddles to work.
- Man & woman gesticulate—talking in a foreign language.
- Kid eats big, hot, sloppy slice of pizza.
- Little woman walks enormous dog.
- Five-year-old coaxes squirrel with lime jelly sandwich.
- Very old man does speed walking while singing Verdi.
- Children play street games (hopscotch, jump rope, tag, penny pitching).

A bridge can also show players moving from one location into another. It can even show players discussing what should happen in the next scene.

Bridges for Large Casts

All bridges enrich the story by giving it another layer. They also involve more participants. If you're working with a dozen people, most of them will get speaking parts. But if you're working with 75 people, some will barely stand out. When all of them have paid to participate, you'd better ask some of them ASAP to "Invent Bridges!" Make sure they get their money's worth by coaching them carefully.

If you shoot 9 scenes, you can easily insert 8 bridges, making a dozen players more visible in the movie. Here's how 75 players can be involved:

- a half dozen are leads
- 2 dozen get smaller parts,
- a dozen are Extras,
- 3 dozen invent Bridges or play into crowd scenes.

In a large group, many won't want to go on camera. Offer them Tech or crew jobs: Production Assistant, continuity, boombox, lights, Grip, sound, storyboard, Assistant Experience Host, publicity, Gofer, cleanup, still photos, refreshments, documentation tape. Many will tell you what they want to do.

Camera placement and lighting awareness are the two "must use" methods to make your audience want to see more. When you can do these, you can stop worrying about price tags on equipment because your tapes will always look expensive.

—Karl Benko

⌘ Choose a bridge

In the scenario "Rest of the Hamptons" by Denise Mourges, we see Belle on her way to a giant fundraising party.

SCENE 5 has been shot: Belle sets her purse on the roof of her car, unlocks the door, and drives off. The purse slides onto the ground, her $500 ticket sticking out (close-up).

SCENE 6 (this you will now shoot): Walking up to the ticket taker, Belle's hand looks in her pocket for her ticket. Pull back: she finds she's lost her purse.

What do you put between Scenes 5 and 6? (choose one):

Option 1: no Bridge at all.

Option 2: 5-second cutaway to pretty fireworks over guests (and nothing happens).

Option 3: 10-second Bridge in which something happens: driving fast, Belle slips a flask out of the glove compartment and takes a swig.*

Option 4: Inside the party, Belle's date asks a couple, "What's happened to Belle?"

Option 5: Belle drives home but finds no purse.

Option 6: The ticket taker welcomes a guest and takes his ticket.

Option 7: A kid on a bike stops where the purse has fallen and reaches down for it.

Answer: I prefer Option 3 because it shows Belle taking risks because she's driving without her pocketbook and no license.

*Caution: This is not an endorsement of reckless behavior. Always ensure the safety of players and staff.

Standards

Don't judge your video by the standards of Hollywood, which can afford to spend $10,000 per minute on any feature bound for the marketplace. We find that by helping players shape their own story and cast it, by leading them in warm-up games and supporting them on camera, we can guarantee them a novel experience and a movie cassette that backs it up.

9 Project Manager Basics

Sound

Starting with your crumby internal mic, test all the mics you own—lavaliere, shotgun, Cardiod...one after another. Test them on the identical sounds, for instance, high pitched scream, portable radio, TV announcer, canary, water spigot, kitchen fan, snoring, dog bark.

Do they pick up what they're supposed to pick up? Do they ignore sounds they're supposed to ignore?

Does the cheapest mic work best? A lot of people in the fast lane forget sound. It gets a lot easier if you have a sure way to test batteries. Do equipment maintenance together & it's not so boring.

Project manager is the job that creates the group. With small groups the Project Manager can also cover the job of Experience Host.

How do I know if I'm a good Project Manager *before* the project starts?

- Do you know a unique space your group would love to visit?
- How about asking a potential sponsor to let your group use space?
- Are you in touch with people who might join your cast?
- Are you realistic about how long events are planned for and how long they really take?
- Can you make your program sound so exciting that people volunteer to work for it?
- Does an ordinary task sound exciting when you describe it?
- Can you happily refund a fee to a customer who says your program is a disaster?

...and *during* the program?

- Can you spot weaknesses in a program—before it crashes?
- Can you invent milestones to show your group where the program is at?
- Whether the budget is $50 or $5000, can you stay within its limits?
- Do you keep enthusiasm up while getting down to nasty details?
- Do you like people even though they vote for the wrong party & belong to the wrong clubs?
- Are you willing to clean a bit so things run more smoothly?
- Can you give a person feedback on a job done wrong without offending him or her?
- Can you supervise staff & volunteers without actually doing their jobs for them?

...and *after* the program?

- Do people trust you with money? Do you keep records of expenses?
- Can you explain why talent releases are needed if your tape is to be aired on cable?
- Do you give credit to others even when most of the credit is due to you?
- Do you expect participants *will* be around next year and *could* come out for another movie?
- When you find the key to upgrading MOVIExperience, will you use it?

If you said yes to most of these questions, you'd make a fine Project Manager for video movies. Let's put you to work.

MOVIExperience with a School

Your little brother has convinced his eleventh-grade class to improvise a video movie. What's your next move?

In this case, the school does the job of Project Manager. It provides equipment and insurance, at least one teacher, a warm, dry meeting place, costumes from the drama department, and a monitor on which to replay the tape. So you're way ahead. Your own Project Manager can focus on locations, warm-ups, & story.

Should you be close to the teacher, to the students, or both? Think of yourself as an advisor: don't do all the work yourself. Make sure people understand the schedule: what the Coach, Camera Operator, and Experience Host (if you have one) will do. Ask them to ask everyone for a story. Get the Screen Test tape going. If the school is paying you a fee, collect that before the session. Or at least submit your bill. At the shoot, watch that the big pieces come together:

- Locations—if they are skimpy, ask players to think of better ones.
- Stories—if you don't like what's coming out of the Brainstorm, ask the Coach to dip into a pool of scenarios. Otherwise dump the story and shoot scenes about a theme.
- Quality of play—if you don't think players are warmed up, run the games again.
- Take II? Help decide whether to shoot again and whether to rewind the tape and delete Take I.
- Your mood—look hopeful, not dubious.

MOVIExperience needs to be done in a short period of time because, after a while, energy fades. The luster of a bright new idea is lost. That's when you put all your energy into finishing things.

—Elisa Abatsis,
Coach, Production Assistant, Assistant Director

Community Shoot

Suppose a group that's made a movie gets publicity and attracts 25 new people who pay $30 each. Is one of them willing to help you in exchange for a freebee? The tasks are clear.

- Give participants receipts and list their names & phone numbers.
- Find a quiet place to Brainstorm where players can also warm up.
- Find a restaurant, lounge, or loft with a TV & VCR to screen the tape.
- Send out a news release that will interest the local press in the project.
- Make sure the Camera Operator checks equipment and batteries & blank tape (and labels tape as soon as possible).
- If the group has too many kids in it or too few, recruit more players to keep a balance.
- Invite well-known storytellers to sit in on the Brainstorm.
- Ask bartenders, storeowners & other local celebrities to join the cast.
- Remind players to bring costumes from home and tag them so they're returned to their owners.

- Before the shoot, ask yourself: can this cast perform this story?

During the shoot, ask:
- Are these players warmed up and ready to go on camera?
- is the Coach or Camera Operator reviewing tape before moving on?
- How many improvs are being shot a second time?
- Who here is from our sponsor, the Press? Do they need to be briefed?
- Is our Experience Host making participants comfortable?
- Are we on time? Should we speed up and not shoot second takes or take our time?

Hold a planning meeting after the session. Discuss:
- Did the session bring you friends, new prospects, potential coaches, or camera people?
- What did we learn to improve our next MOVIExperience?

College Shoot

Here are ways to involve more than one class or discipline in your project.
- Creative Writing class invents stories.
- Publicity class furnishes press releases and follow-up.
- Music seminar offers original audio cassettes for a boombox during scenes.
- Theatre class gathers props, hats & costume pieces.
- Carpentry class upgrades locations you've chosen.
- Production class turns the story your group selects into a storyboard.
- Video department sends one shooter to cover the story and a second to document the entire process—editing both tapes in studio so you get a comprehensive tape with titles and credits.

In choosing a college cast, keep in mind your movie will bring out students from departments that have nothing to do with each other. The administration loves this cross-pollination: Nurses find themselves improvising with law students, German students with chemists. At the screening bring all these groups together.

Once you're accepted by the college, make friends at the Alumni Association. There may be a need for your services to shoot a story for the reunion of a college class.

MOVIExperience for Seniors

Three things I've learned working with seniors:

- Talk loud and don't rush.
- Instead of asking players to move for the camera, ask the camera to move for them.
- Be willing to shoot a fantasy that was popular decades ago.

There's a strong undercurrent of feeling in senior centers. At one I noticed a man and a woman who were treating each other like total strangers; I learned they had been married for 60 years. At another a man did an insulting improv with a woman who was cooking him breakfast. Later the social worker explained to me that his wife had died the week before.

Figure 24. Nursing home interaction in Brooklyn, New York.
Peter and Lynn Bernfield sing the story that the seniors want
to hear. Photo credit: Author.

Churches & Temples

Don't publicize the event. Invite all guests as if you're throwing a birthday or an anniversary party. Make it sound important; you believe it is important. Why: 12 to 25 people will share a unique and intimate experience that's available nowhere else. In a protected environment, they'll ventilate longings, goals, jokes, values that we often take for granted. Working as a brand-new team, they'll forge, out of many opinions, one dramatic belief about a favorite theme. This will be our scenario.

Some will stand back and watch. Give them Tech jobs that guarantee they do have an *experience*. By supervising carefully, you can keep your standards high.

Others will play themselves in the role for which they are cast. Still others will drop their own identities to step into an unfamiliar role. Have training games ready for them. The most enthusiastic players may move from function to function—and also play two parts.

Another Dimension

Players on the sidelines may be asked what they expect of the next scene, and their guesses will be recorded on the documentation tape. At the end of the day, this cassette will be screened first—before the cassette on which our story is recorded.

Advantages to Working in Churches & Temples

Problems coming up in the shoot are handled easily because people feel they're in a family. They're all insiders. The Brainstorm goes smoothly because familiar points of view are being shared. Players are willing to reveal more of themselves because they feel no one present is a stranger. The possibility of planning a second MOVIExperience is greater because it's an excuse for this moviemaking family to meet again.

Caution

Carefully inviting participants doesn't guarantee that you reach those who can turn out a *movie* while having a delicious *experience*. Gauge potential guests on the basis of:

- known talents for improv, debating, performing
- tolerance for new games, programs
- playfulness and humor

Make participants feel they've been handpicked. They're special, doing special work for a video piece, which won't be shown on PBS but will hold special insights. The format is special and was developed under special conditions.

We give out special thanks, in the form of an R & D Certificate. Through the day we show clips of past tapes edited so they fit into free moments. About the shoot, we can say, "You will never forget it."

⌘ Test yourself

What would you do?

- A player is upset by a very active exercise: what do you do?

  _____

- A player objects to not getting the lead: what can you do?

  _____

- A player has to go home for an hour: what do you do?

  _____

How would you respond to these misfortunes?

- The camcorder breaks down; what should happen?

  _____

- The weatherman is wrong, and it rains on your park scene. What are your options?

  _____

- Your VCR starts eating up the tape; what can be done. ?

  _____

Here's some flak you might get from participants.

- "Why can't I drink a six-pack during the shoot?"
- "I don't like the way this is going, so I want my money back."
- "I refuse to be in your movie if that scene is not erased."

Even if you may not love it, accept the scenario the group comes up with—unless of course:

- it's violent, pornographic, libelous, or
- it will lead to such confusion the footage will be useless, or
- it can't be shot since key players & locations are not available, or
- it stars a few participants and leaves all the others out.

Be assertive; it's better to grab a mediocre decision with confidence than waffle while searching for the ideal solution.

Keep involving people in decisions again and again so they're impressed with the result—it's their own creation! Highlight contributions by participants; soft-pedal staff contributions. I believe any close group that uses the MOVIExperience approach can make a video movie that ends up on cable and on many bookshelves.

√ Checklist before managing a project	
Planning	What standards do you want to meet, for example, for audio volume or costumes?
	What style—fast cuts, slow pans, zooms, move the camera?
	What mode—Linear, How to Tell, Thematic, Team Play, Camera Writes the Scenario?
	Schedule—intensive two-day shoot, one week? 4 three-hour sessions?
	Where will the tape be shown—on cable, at homes, in video stores, festivals?
	Who will pay production costs—cast or sponsors?
	Is your meeting place within walking distance to locations? Do you need a car?
Office work	Who will dupe & distribute a list of phone numbers of cast and staff?
Equipment:	Camcorder(s), battery charger, mic, tripod, lighting
Expenses	Equipment, transportation, phone, mailing, copying, studio edit & dupes, cell phone in field, insurance?
Income	Sponsorship by an organization, local businesses, families, players. Fees paid by participants. Sale of dupes, a t-shirt, workshops?
Training	Classes offered locally, in media classes, training by mail? Training over the weeks before the session, the day before the session?
Aids	Snacks, drinks, a pool of props, costumes; orientation materials: handouts, reviews, frequently asked questions (FAQ), cassettes of other movies.
Edit	Will you edit in camera or keep all takes and scan over the bad ones during the screening? Will you edit in studio later or on a home computer? Edit only to clean up tape, add titles & credits?
Evaluation	By whom? Of player group, staff, equipment, format? How is the evaluation used?
Costs	If you already have equipment and a phone, if you limit the length of your program, a video movie can be made for a few hundred dollars raised from sponsors and participants. With a volunteer in-studio editor, you don't need much more.

10 The Experience Host

Nonverbal Improv

Take turns playing nonverbally for the camera. Each player has 3 minutes to fill.

Fill them by running at the camera from a distance or emptying your pockets close-up, putting on clothes, playing drums, greeting teammates nonverbally.

Those playing off camera can add birdcalls, sound effects, song, or dialogue, laughter—all *ad lib.*

On playback see for how many seconds each segment keeps our interest & why.

Participants who don't need to go on camera can handle this common sense role without training. All they need is a liking for people and copies of the frequently asked questions, which you can copy and hand out.

The Experience Host is a key person who says, "I'm here to make you comfortable making movies."

Many who come to the MOVIExperience have exasperating jobs and monotonous home lives. They embrace what we've got for them because we give them energy. That energy begins with the Experience Host, most likely the first person they meet.

The excited people who come out for a video movie, what do they really want? A few come because something new is being offered. Some want to learn improv, because it builds confidence, speeds up response time, unleashes hidden feelings, lubricates the imagination...

Some long to see what they look like on tape. Some need to fill empty Wednesday nights; loneliness drives them to you. Or they're preparing for a stint in standup comedy. Some come if their pal comes. They don't if the pal doesn't.

Most are searching for a friend or mate.

Frequently Asked Questions

Question: Will our movie be shown on network?

Answer: No. To shoot broadcast quality tape would make it impossible for us to do what we do: shape our own video movie and within a few hours screen it for our own pleasure and our sense of accomplishment.

Q: How long will our movie run?

A: About 20 minutes—not including screen tests, interviews, and shots of players improvising at locations.

Q: Why improvise?

A: So we don't have to write and rewrite a script. So we can work off a scenario, a structure loose enough to reflect the ideas of many players. Our lines will not have to be memorized; they'll sound fresh. Because we'll build characters from personal experience, they'll appear livelier.

Q: Why a scenario?

A: It points to the purpose of each scene but allows the cast to fill in details their own way.

Q: How can I look good on camera?

A: Choose a part that's close to what you do in real life. Play it with plenty of feeling. Warm up before the shoot and keep breathing while you're on camera.

Q: What's MOVIExperience mean?

A: It means you get to influence every decision that goes into making a movie: scouting locations, screen tests, Brainstorm, casting, warm-ups, the shoot, and the screening.

Q: Where will our movie be seen?

A: It will be screened here, shown on cable or at festivals and duped for everyone who wants to show it at home.

Explaining the Experience Host Role

Here is what the Experience Host is thinking: "Greetings I am the Experience Host. I make sure people are having a good time experiencing moviemaking whether they're warming up in character or looking at some great video that shows how we work, learning how to hold a mic boom and clamp-on spot or getting made up. If they want to shoot a little, I can free up a video camera, and they can even direct what they shoot. For players who want to know more about what we do, I screen some short tapes. When other questions come up, I answer them or get the answers. There are a dozen skills that go into moviemaking—from drawing a storyboard to giving out prizes for the best dialogue and the most vivid character. I make sure everyone has as many of these experiences as possible.

Figure 25. Screening.

"I work to make players feel comfortable. I give players positive feedback when they come from the shoot.

"I also find out what players are thinking and relay that to Coach & Project Manager. This is what I need to know:

- Does everyone understand what we're doing right now?
- Is the temperature OK, the bathroom clean? Are the costumes together?
- Does anyone here want to shoot another MOVIExperience? If so, can they get their hands on a camcorder?
- Is my energy strong? Am I being clear, positive, responsive?

"I'm also the one who gives prizes after the screening—for improvisation, costume, characterization, comedy, and whatever else we decide is important.

"I organize a cleanup, and when I find participants who want to make another video movie, I get them together with our Coach, Camera Operator, and Project Manager."

⇒✎ Making the documentation tape

- Free the camcorder from time to time to give participants the experience of using it to enrich the shoot. Help them shoot each other doing one-minute interviews. Their footage, on the documentation tape, is played back before screening the story tape.

Figure 26. Free up the camcorder for players to use. Jackie di Chiara's footage documents the book-signing party for this book. Photo credit: Claudia Gere.

Types of Players You'll Be Meeting

When you look over your group, how many of these people will you recognize?

Stabilizers

Stabilizers work a lifetime to develop a comfortable identity. This they've achieved in spite of bad upbringing, abuse, relocation, attacks by classmates, extended unemployment, punishing affairs, problematic marriage, lethal job. They take few risks. What they hoped to be in life is expressed in numbers—of children, CDs, orgasms, years married, insurance policies carried, trips to Disneyland. If you can get Stabilizers to play, the one role they'll do is themselves.

Wafflers

Wafflers must change. They hate to be dependent on 1 job, 1 mate, 1 hobby. Because they flit, they acquire solid information about behavior, ethnicity, rituals, the FBI. They enjoy risk—playing difficult roles with abandon. But when they're needed (at rehearsal, meeting or shoot), do not count on them. Why don't they show? A distant cousin dies? Their cat gets sick? Neighbors steal their 7-foot boa? They have a fight and must spend all day making up? They forgot (that's a real one). They overslept (a big one). They have a migraine (a very big one). The babysitter didn't show (quite popular). Exhausted (overused). They decided our theories are incorrect (used in New Jersey). They feel I'm irritable (easy). And since I'm to blame, they do not phone. If you want one Waffler to come out, invite at least five.

No-Nos

No-Nos may come on time and stay to the end, but they question what happens. A single can of beer or lit cigarette sparks protest. "The dip has onions in it! Yuck!" Warm-up music is too loud, soft, fast, slow...lights are too bright, dim, hot, yellow...the program is too vague, explicit, boring, bold. Yet I've seen a No-No take over, after scrutinizing me for 3 hours, and run a session for the last half-hour— positively. No-Nos cannot be dismissed—because there are so many millions of them, and because they do reveal ways to strengthen our program.

Pros

Pros earn thousands (or hundreds) doing what most participants do for the love of it. How do they behave? They show up. They're on time. They stay until the end of the session. During the improv they ask for a specific task. If they feel they can't bring it off, they ask for another task right away. They demand conditions under which they'll perform that task: the right partner, costume, lights, music. They *refuse* to come off looking badly.

Sky Jumpers

Sky Jumpers have stayed out of the limelight for years, while urging themselves: "Take the leap. Sing! Dance! Tell a joke!" Give them something easy; they do well. Praise them; they don't believe you. They may not want to play again. They figure: "I survived. Once is enough."

Celebrity Hounds

You may not be a celebrity, but you can be made into one. The Celebrity Hound decides that Tuesday evenings you are the most famous person they know. Details of your past suddenly make you important in their eyes. By hanging out with you, they too become important. They create a sun in whose light they bask, and that sun is you.

Thin Skins

Thin Skins do fine with 10 or 15 in the group, but if it dwindles to 4 or 5, they vanish. In front of 15 people they don't mind revealing themselves. But in a small group they ask themselves: "If I did a scene with that Loser with the hairpiece over there, what would the girl who's wearing the Eileen Fisher outfit think?...If I improvised with the fatty sitting next to me, she'd make me into her daughter, and I'd never have a mother that fat, so I don't even want to be here anymore. Thank you very much."

Goofs

Goofs need to joke around & rap with each other. If asked to fit in and play a scene, they're turned off. Our activity is no longer fun. At a Valentine's Day theme party, a Goof was asked to play a Roman soldier. He declined, explaining the material was too heavy. Like the upper class, Goofs expect life to be wonderful. If it's not, what's happening around them is wrong. They split.

Gratefuls

Gratefuls don't expect anything of themselves or of the project. They enjoy a parade of people and of people playing people. They don't need to shine. Mainly they want to spend a couple of hours in a social environment where things bubble and pop. It's more interesting than the 11 p.m. news. Gratefuls give feedback without malice or flattery.

Free-Players

Free-players see improvisation as exploration. In Chicago, according to Eric Forsberg, many men at age 31, with stable jobs on car lots or in insurance, ask themselves what they're missing. They sign up for an improv workshop that takes them off their path. Their trip leads to a more playful way of being, a theatrical role far outside their personal experience plus intimate encounters with people they never thought existed. They don't need to quit their job for standup comedy. They don't train to play *Hamlet*. They look to probe their identity, marriage, childhood, and coming maturity. The last time I saw Eric, I asked him if women are part of this scheme. He thought a while, having just been married, and said, "Maybe."

Serious Players

These are the folk who are desperately tired of being themselves. They come to you because they know you're not going to mock them for putting on a dress or pasting down a moustache. At home they'd get the silent treatment even for using an English accent. Here they can make surreal leaps into elves, pirates, spirits, extra-celestials, humanoids, pharaohs, czarinas. Protect them even when they fail, because they grasp the essence of play.

Do you have your own type? Add it.

Who Might Show Up in Your Group

Members have something in common but are also diverse. For instance, they all come from the same block but have different social backgrounds.

Nobody is under 10 years old, unless they've been checked out by a staff person.

There are no complainers because staff encourages people who don't enjoy the program to go home. Refunds are given early in the session.

A few members are professional; they arrive on time and are careful about props and costumes. They make sure they know the Coach's Signal that's being used. If their scene seems weak, they ask to redo it.

A few players have tech skills. They know how many watts can be loaded on a circuit and how to position spot lights and microphones. They get rid of *hot spots* on the set and they can set up a VCR and TV. They like to solve problems.

A few players have a vivid sense of story; they add the key scene to a scenario the group has invented.

Players who come into the group by chance (for instance through an ad) have a sense of adventure. They're ready to meet others who also like to play characters and explore situations.

Players from the same family can play across genders and ages: Aunt Phyllis plays Uncle Steve as a boy. Rodney plays his Mom talking to the principal about too much homework. Beth and Allie, who are married to George and Jupiter, play George and Jupiter talking about how Beth and Allie play cards or go sightseeing.

Figure 27. Marybeth Home, Experience Host for "Ball of the Friends & Lovers."

Guarantee Players the Experience They Want

What we're offering makes MOVIExperience different from any other program. You can:

- operate the camera before and after the shoot
- handle microphones
- position lights
- make decisions about how a location can shape up on camera
- help choose the scenario and tweak it until it makes sense
- play the character you've wanted to do since you were a kid
- pick a costume from somebody's closet and flaunt it
- bring the prop that helps you slip into your role
- figure out ways to play a second character on camera
- learn the same improv games that are used by professionals
- hang out with people who share your curiosity & sense of fun
- see the movie you've made immediately after you make it
- give or get a prize for the strongest qualities of the video.

11 Writing Improv Scenarios

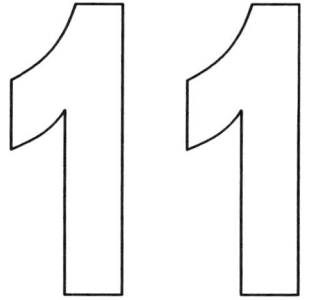

Review

If you've been driving in the Fast Lane, look what you have experience to do now:

- zoom
- pan
- tilt
- cover a party
- lead and shoot a game
- record 2 shots in motion
- voice your opinion
- strip your tape of bad footage
- live without dialog

Your team has the skills to grab a story of 3–4 scenes, go shoot it, and then return to the book.

What keeps a story from rambling or bogging down is a *scenario*. A good story is expressed not in words or ideas but in actions detailed by a scenario. The scenario is the guts of any improv movie. To launch a video of 20 to 45 minutes, all you need is a scenario of about 250 good words.

Never underestimate the power of a scenario.

Using Spines

I call a short version of the scenario a *spine*. If a dozen players are searching for a scenario to shoot, you'll probably get several spines. Here's Deb Lacusta's spine for "The August."

Some negative people are drawn to a guru who convinces them the world will come to an end August 1.

You know this trip, don't you? It's a comedy about unhappiness. "The August" was improvised twice—in Chicago and in New York City. (See the full scenario in Chapter 14.)

A Spine can tell us roughly how many players are required, what ages & genders, what kind of locations, and whether we'll be shooting in daylight or at night. Take look at the spine for Pat Mew's "2 Families":

> *A teenage girl and her parents are in such conflict that she refuses to talk to them. Down the block a correct but childless couple puts up a sign: "If you want to be adopted, call this number."*

Depending on how many players you have, this story can branch out to the relatives and neighbors of both families, to social workers, therapists, even the police and the courts. (See the full scenario in Chapter 14.)

Movies on film require a hundred times more detail. Every camera angle, every move, word, sound effect, costume piece, set design, prop, and nuance is conceived and packed into a shooting script hundreds of pages long, written over the years—usually by one person.

If we waited for a shooting script, you'd never get the experience of creating your own story—through improvisation. You could never ask for a part tailored to your skills. And you'd never enjoy, within hours, the many experiences that go into moviemaking.

Leave Endings Open

That's why our movies start with a Brainstorm (see Chapter 3), where you shape the *same story that you'll shoot,* and invent the *same parts you want to play.* Here's what a Brainstorm does:

- breaks out your story into locations where people will interact
- suggests activities to give players focus
- tells what happens between players—but not how the scene must end

For instance, a sales manager calls one of his busy saleswomen into his office. The manager reads a report that critiques her work; she opens her appointment book. The manager warns about a slump in profits. *Will she be laid off or not?* The scene can end several ways.

A homeless woman visits her daughter to be put up for a week. The mother fumbles for a sandwich in her sack; the daughter is taking a course on TV and complains she was homeless as a child. *Will she take her mother in or refuse?*

A wife stops her husband in front of a dress display. She reads price tags and labels; he studies the inside of his wallet. They discuss what he spends at the bar. *Does she get a dress or not?*

A woman complains to her friend about losing a file in her studio office. She looks under the bed while her friend offers to help her clean up. The friend begins sweeping every paper off the desk onto the floor while the woman screams, "Stop!" *Is the file found? Does the studio get clean?*

Figure 28. "Jonah Complex" at Cross Currents, Chicago—the Nineveh Story, using a game from ImprovOlympix (1981). Photo credit: Virgil Schrock.

Guidelines for Writing Stories for Video

- Know ten times more about your characters than the viewer will ever know.
- Get rid of characters that are all bad (or all good) because they will fail to surprise us. And the core of any scenario is surprise.
- Since a story is often about difficulties that prevent leading characters from reaching their goals, make these goals sympathetic.

- Keep asking, as you grow your story: "Do we have the cast we need to shoot this? Can we find the locations?"
- Get our interest.
  - Involve us intimately in your characters' lives and goals.
  - Use plenty of action—but justified so it makes sense.
  - Once a character's behavior is set, change it, but invent a good reason to do so.
  - Present to us, in a believable way, what we don't expect.

⌘ **Grabbing interest**

Start the *first* story you can think of to grab the interest of fellow players. How long can you hold onto that interest? (Somebody hold a watch.) If your story loses interest before you reach an ending, players raise their hands. If a majority of hands are up, it's the next player's turn to grab.

Portray leading characters as three-dimensional (not as cartoons). Make them sympathetic or potentially sympathetic. Give us clear alternatives about what can happen. Arouse our curiosity; then satisfy it.

Here's a real story that keeps our interest: It was in the *New York Times* that I learned of a fireman's daughter, who at age 17 leaves home in a family car. She drives straight through to Tompkins Square, New York City, calmly steps out into a sea of homeless people & addicts. Her frantic parents follow her to the city. Dad pastes posters in all firehouses—announcing her disappearance. Meanwhile the girl makes friends, drifts excitedly from one pad to another. Her mother, looking fixedly for her, *doesn't recognize her* the first time they pass on a sidewalk. The girl seems totally at ease, unselfconscious. Sometime after her return home, she confides in friends: she can't wait to get lost again.

⌘ **Try True Story**

Ask players to skim newspapers or magazines at home and pick out a story. Write it up as a scenario with scene locations and actions. If no newspaper story comes to light, adapt a story from family history—or from memory.

Beginnings & Ends

Stand in a circle. Agree on one sentence for the beginning and one for the ending of a story. Going clockwise, take turns fleshing out the middle of the story.

⌘ Try Beginnings & Ends

At noon, ten-year-old Jo has a fight with her parents and leaves home.... At midnight, Jo returns. Fill in what happens between noon & midnight.

Using Themes

If you can't agree on a scenario, then brainstorm themes, list them, and vote to choose your favorite. Develop it into a dozen short scenes, which will not have to be as carefully interwoven as in a scenario.

Figure 29. 700 A.D., St. Patrick escapes slavery and walks 200 miles across Ireland: story opening for "Video Holiday" (1995). Credit: Morgan McGivern.

Love

Sketch scenes about love of money, love of kids, love of parents, love of rebellion, love of risk, love of romance...For instance:

- character in love with money is discovered recycling dental floss and paper plates
- old man in love with kids crawls on the floor, splashed with water bombs as he tells enchanting fables
- woman in love with her mother satisfies endless demands at the same time she tells Mom what the score is
- boy's love of rebellion is characterized by his revolutionary clothes, his macho tone, and his need to quarrel with the most innocent remarks of friends
- love of risk on a beach is dramatized by a life guard's loud shark warnings, which the swimmer ignores
- love of romance makes two infatuated people have such a strong fantasy about each other, neither can see who the other person really is

Fame

To dramatize this theme, show us unknown people who suddenly become famous, haughty people who assume fame is in their blood, teenagers who would risk anything to be famous, people who hate themselves because fame passed them by, snobbish servants who take menial jobs to be close to the famous...

Can a group find *the* story for it?

Howard Jerome says that, as a performer on stage, he's often overwhelmed by the enormous tide of creativity rushing at him from out of the audience. "I'm a pretty creative guy," he observes, "but there are a hundred times more stories, poems, scenes, songs out there than in me. The problem is how to focus that life-based energy, bring it forward, and frame it so the people it comes from become aware of it."

Finding the story is the problem we've been working on for 49 years. When we offer MOVIExperience for a fee to a Sponsor, and agree to deliver it within a set time, we'd better solve this problem. Otherwise the creativity of the group will drown us under clipboards, spotlights, and camcorders. Individuals will come up with a storm of ideas and will disagree about how to use our precious minutes.

That's why we meet players for 2 or 3 hours at a Brainstorm before the shoot.

Cupid Work

Exactly how did your mother & father meet? Make that your story. Show all the forces separating them (in which case you would not be born) and the force that brought them together. The movie *Back to the Future* spells this theme out.

Example: A man & woman meet when their cars collide. After accusations & despair, they go about repairing the damage. Making the best of it, they help each other handle mechanics and insurance claims. Discovering each other's strengths and weaknesses, they come to enjoy each other, get married, and bring three kids into the world. (True Story.)

Searching for his blind date, a man throws quarters into a public phone to find where she might be, then scouts bar after bar. The blind date, meanwhile, is in a dark movie theatre with a big bag of popcorn. She's forgotten about her date, but he's destined to find her. They have two children. (True Story.)

Using Clichés

Al Ramos explains using clichés: "MOVIExperience is developing nicely, but it's not funny enough. It's not movie enough. Let's shoot phonier movie formulas. Such clichés are constantly being created in our national fantasyland by you, the audience. For instance, *Fatal Attraction* sported a neat, believable ending before you, the public, were invited to screen it. You said, 'Change it; the ending is too neat.' You preferred this:

"The villainess (Glenn Close) sinks under bath water for 2 minutes (a superhuman length of time), then pops out of the tub like a banshee with a carving knife in her hand. The wife (Anne Archer) shoots this demon in the heart, thus healing her marriage, while the husband (Michael Douglas) is made aware of her quiet powers.

"Here are some phony movie moments I scribbled down on the subway. Please add your own."

Sly Jock

He tells shy girl how pretty she is, how he's fallen in love with her dimple...Now all she has to do is come up to his apartment; she believes him.

Cliché Gangster

A gangster threatens to kill delivery boy unless the boy reveals where a rival gangster is. Boy blurts out, "33rd Street." Gangster turns toward 33rd Street, pauses to shoot delivery boy, then rushes on.

Naïve Girl

Girl is warned to get out of the building where the Purple Power has killed her boyfriend. As if dazed, she pays no attention. She steps numb—through scarlet shadows and squeaking doors—because she must avenge her love. And we in the audience follow her—breathless.

Idealist

Recent college graduate makes detailed plans to clean corruption out of the Mayor's office, top to bottom.

Last-Minute Reprieve

As the prisoner is led to the electric chair, a panting messenger arrives with the governor's pardon.

Monster

A monster eats a whole human being, then pulls a mouse to bits.

Soft-Hearted Soldier

Surrounded by his dead buddies, a soldier looks toward enemy lines and shouts: "I'm going to kill you, every one of you . . !"

Showoff

Encouraging a nerd to take a big risk, the showoff says, "It's easy. I've done it many times. What are you waiting for? Show the kind of stuff you're made of." Nerd takes his advice, goes ahead, and meets disaster.

Fat Millionaire and Alluring Pickpocket

She puts him at ease, shows him how much she likes him, asks him what he'd like to do, laughs, kisses him... until he's been relieved of his wallet and keys.

Charlton Heston

The plantation owner destroys millions of invading ants—alone. As he returns from the battle, mopping his brow, Mexican underlings leap to their feet and applaud his machismo.

Try adding a favorite movie cliché to your next video movie.

Al Ramos contributed this section. Ramos is an accomplished producer for both stage and video contributing weekly to Manhattan Cable.

Using Locations

You can shoot your *whole movie in one location*—a park, for instance, where there are dozens of little locations inside the big one. Cutting down on the distance you move cast and equipment will save headaches. (See page 18.)

If you've found great locations, and you can't figure out how to match them to scenes, let your leads relate to each other as they *go from one location to another* (they will find good reasons to do so). Your story will go with them.

Try giving players *the same activity*—such as playing a slot machine or cooking a stew. Nonverbal contrasts will be interesting to the viewer.

Try getting several players into *the same emotion:* shoot members of different families, for instance, as they approach the same fresh grave, or the same icy wave.

As for a *single location*: shoot the wall of the same tunnel, for instance. First put a group of ten-year-olds listening to the echo, then senior citizens with flash cameras, then workers stringing fiber optic. Exploration makes strong, interesting video.

Favorite Formats

Familiar and basic sequences of scenes surround us. Take these accepted happenings and create characters by making them relevant to your life. Here are the structures; make them your own.

Boy Meets Girl

How boy meets girl must be the favorite of all time. How would this story play out for you? What do you see when you ask yourself: "Who is the boy, the girl? How do they meet? How does he lose her? Where do they come together again?" If you close your eyes and visualize scenes from your story, these questions can be answered in your imagination. If your boy has only one leg and your girl is a part-time butcher, you have the makings of an interesting story.

Big Changes

Choose the most stable group you can think of; then stand it on its head. For example, when a big real estate agent is fired, his complacent family is paralyzed. He gets a job at a hotdog stand, then as a janitor, then at a phone-answering service. His wife weeps. His kids scoff. Then they all realize: nothing is sure; the search for work and a roof over your head is endless. They all start behaving like Dad, and the family comes together again.

Day of the Life

Pick anyone powerful or mysterious, with a complex routine. Peek into this life every two hours or so, making sure your lead is *not* in every scene (give him a rest!). A good subject is a mayor, who gets enormous respect at city hall but none at home, visiting with firemen, bankers, celebrities, victims of accidents, opponents, society dames. The ending is simple: an alarm wakes the lead up just as it did exactly 24 hours before.

The Search

An individual or group sets out to find something: a helpful consultant, fortuneteller, medical specialist, sum of money, lost heirloom, secret code, missing cat. During their search, players meet strange people and have unforeseen experiences. Either they reach their goal in triumph, or they discover it was senseless (for example, *Treasure of the Sierra Madre*).

Mounting Disaster

Hollywood has the resources to shoot a *Towering Inferno*, but you don't need skyscraper and flames to shoot this premise. You can create mounting danger and hysteria in a business that's going bankrupt or a home where disease is spreading. Dramatize the mysterious onset of the sickness, the doctor's visits, attempts at quarantine, gossip in the neighborhood, a second case, panic, how family members treat each other... and what they've learned when it's all over.

The Trip

The trip depends on finding locations that suggest your players are moving great distances. Actually all locations must be close to each other, so you can meet players at one location, shoot, then move to another location where you meet other players right away.

Here's your chance to shoot the family planning an ambitious trip and then outfitting themselves at the mall—easy scenes. Use traveling footage from a moving car, scary nights in motels, enormous picnics where all forks and spoons have been forgotten, expensive tents filled with insects, hot-dog stands with impressive skylines in the background.

How-To

How to behave in a singles crowd, for instance; how to protest the closing of a school; how to make a killing in the stock market.

How to Get Married is different from *Getting Married*. In the first story *every moment is examined:* will the woman expect the man to dress up or down, to sleep together or apart? Will the parents approve? If not, will the couple change plans? How do the lovers decide where to honeymoon? How does the bride buy a wedding dress? What mishaps happen at the wedding rehearsal? All these tiny events lead to the main event: they *do* get married, and this is how they did it.

Role Switch

A toilet attendant inherits millions; a warden becomes an inmate. See the old *Freaky Friday* with role switchers Barbara Harris & Jody Foster; it's about a mother-and-daughter switch.

Using Frameworks

Here are seven frameworks that can be used for an interesting MOVIExperience.

Go Location to Location

For now forget bedroom, living room, or kitchen. Don't try inventing stories about people who live there. Instead go to places that offer many times more activity, happening, and atmosphere. For instance:

- A smoky pool hall is where a girl leaving for college has her last game of pool with her steady boyfriend.
- A high-class florist is where a bevy of woman travelers laugh about the smells of Haiti when the girl with ribbons and wrapping paper is herself Haitian.
- A city dump is stacked with rusty computers where two hackers are searching for a part that they can't afford to buy.
- A $5 barber shop is a place to instruct the barber how to give you a $20 haircut.
- An auto-wrecker's lot is where a guy is working his way to a degree in psych.

What does an Anthrax lab say to you, a dry drinking fountain, a laptop that shows movies, a Web page from Afghanistan? Instead of a scene demanding a location, a location can tell you what your story is about.

Go from Group to Group

Put players into 3 groups—each with the same hobby or age. Or let players choose what group they want to join: cool grandparents, fast-moving young adults, jaded teenagers?

Provide them all with a common focus. In *Family Reunion* it was a couple whose child is dying of cancer. All players took an outright stand—for or against chemotherapy. The kid unwittingly became a star—as everybody wondered whether or not he would be alive next year.

Another framework: the community meeting, where members have lifelong friendships and grudges to settle. Another is the mental institution—doctors, nurses, patients.

These are examples of the team mode. The camera doesn't terminate an improv; it simply picks up another improv nearby. Coaches alert the Camcorder Operator when a group is getting hot, if it wants to move and where.

Go from Home to Home

Get permission to use your rich cousin's house, or the apartment with 17 cats, or the old couple's trailer. Some of your hosts can be themselves on camera. Your story is a travelogue through the day-to-day habits of the wealthy, broke, snobbish, ethnic—including the refugee in the tar shack and the young folks with the 50-foot swimming pool.

What holds your story together? Any person common to all the homes—a real estate agent, babysitter, oil-burner man. How does it end? Whether it ends in dispute, misunderstanding, sudden friendship or a big picnic, you'll have plenty of scenes to set up and shoot.

Who We Are

What went on between us & our parents to make us do what we do today? For instance, during the eighties the newspaper was full of stories about 30-year-olds coming home to live. They couldn't afford the style of living they were used to.

We've shot their story, *Boomerang Kids*, three times, but we've never dealt with the big question: what did the parents do to make kids who boomerang ten years later? Wasn't Dad strict enough?

Didn't he teach self-reliance? Did he himself collapse when the going got rough?

And what did Mom do: play bridge, distrust the neighbors, assign the kids tasks that could not be done?

Depending on whether your cast numbers 10 or 25, scenes with relatives and neighbors happen naturally as soon as the kids return home. This part of your scenario has been written: it's about memories of the past.

What happens if the parents leave the kids to take care of themselves? This you can discover by jumping ahead: shoot breakfast next week. Who buys the food? Who's doing the cooking?

At 4 a.m. a month from now, who will be sleepless? Why? You don't need to write a scenario to answer these questions. They are answered by the players as the improv goes *one of many possible ways.*

Fortunes

Briefly describe what we want to be doing in 10 years; then shoot what we think that will look like. 50 kids from S. E. Polk High School, Iowa picked this scenario.

Some chose to show how the worm turns. A boy who's been snubbed for years by a girl becomes an electronics millionaire. Now when she wants him to exchange teen memories, he tells her politely a plane is waiting for him; he doesn't have the time.

In Iowa they used makeup to bridge the gap between age 18 and 30. Three of the 50 participants were busy all day with cold cream, liner, and lipstick. Not all the players looked 30, but they all played 30 with a vengeance. A 10-year jump ahead into your fortune will work for you as well.

Coffee Took Me There

Suppose one player drinks super-strong coffee at bedtime, which sends him on a walk, where he's invited to share a six-pack, after which he goes to sleep in a car, which takes him to a circus with cotton candy.... Suppose other players are also affected by memory flashes, giant chocolate bars, pop, a stack of hamburgers, or something else that changes their behavior.

The scenario is a comedy about people who have no will of their own. If the World Series is on, they have no choice; they must watch the World Series.

Dreams

All cast members play a character in the dream of one player. Continue, one after the other, until you've collected the group's dream life on video.

The Five Ws

A conventional way to base a story is by defining Who, What, Where, When and Why. Let's see how this works out in Jackie Di Chiara's "27 Years on the Bottom Rung."

Who: A vivacious and headstrong woman enters a relationship with an uptight, avaricious man

What: The Problem: She gets the impression that his politics and lifestyle make more sense than hers.

Where: Their two homes—visited by her friends and their babies; parks, restaurant, workplaces.

When: Over a stretch of 27 years with constant doubt, leading up to the woman's serious sickness.

Why: This is for the actress to justify: the man has greater self-confidence than she does, or she needs to serve a man like her own father.

Raising the Stakes

One evening after 10 years the man offers to marry her! She accepts. She also invites an old boyfriend to spend the night with her. Next day she confesses to her fiancé that she was unfaithful, and he calls off the engagement. Before moving out of town, her father offers his home to the couple, but the fiancé says it's not quite right for him and turns it down. There are dozens of other ways the stakes can be raised. See if you can add three, for example, put pressure on the woman to think better of herself, get free of her habits and break her relationship. How can the situation change before year 27 rolls around? If you keep raising the stakes, your public will be on the edge of their chairs for most of the story.

Character in Story

The secret of character is to establish a set of behaviors and actions fast as you can. Then contradict those behaviors and justify the change. In the story above, the uptight guy can be shown skimping and squeezing pennies. But then he offers the girl marriage. He could be a secret benefactor with a heart of steel.

12 Coach in the Field

What most improvs do (just as in real-life encounters) is move players forward on the track of *their relationship*.

We want to see not a dead end but change. As Coach you can make change likely before you shoot. Remind players:

- where the story is, where it could go, and how it could get there
- of their feelings, attitudes, goals
- are they in focus; are they in the here and now?

In every scene, make one participant your assistant. Before running the scene tell him or her what the problems are, what Coach's Signal you plan to use, what possible outcomes the scene has.

Share your authority to give others the *experience* of moviemaking. Give them the sense that they could soon be shooting their own story without you.

Changing Signals

Pause action by tapping the Camera Operator on the shoulder. To keep continuity, tap at the end of a sentence.

Suppose the scene is about Charlie asking his grandmother Lucinda to invest in a new dot-com business. What's the Signal to use? Here are some techniques and when to use them.

Overlap

Overlap is useful when people meet; it might boost the energy like this:

CHARLIE (low pitched & slow): Grandma, you look great! And you're moving so gracefully. Who would know you had a hip operation last year? I can't even tell which hip it was. Are you taking your calcium pills?

LUCINDA at the same time (fast and high pitched): Charlie, you are bad. You never write, you never call, and the only time I see you is when you need a favor. I used to babysit for you when your parents ran off to the movies; we were so close back then.

Figure 30. Troy and Silvana use games to boost their energy level.

5-Second Delay

When the pace needs to be slowed, 5-Second Delay is useful. Here's how that might sound:

CHARLIE: Here's the prospectus I told you about, Grandma.

LUCINDA: (clearing her throat) Now you're going to ask me for one of my famous thousand-dollar bills.

CHARLIE: (laughs) Big businessmen are begging to invest in us.

LUCINDA: (points to a line) Where'd you get such confidence from, boy?

CHARLIE: (bowing slowly) From you, Grandma.

The next time you pause the action, you can change the Signal again. If you like what's happening between the players, use no Signal at all.

⌘ A fast character game

Choose a location. Every player plays the character farthest away from him and at your signal plays himself again. For instance, players all play their parents, then themselves, then their kids (or kids they could have), then themselves, then an animal that's like their character... a hijacker... a mayor...

Take II

Ask players to warm up before their scene so they'll be hot when they go on camera. If a scene is failing, call, "cut!" and ask the Camera Operator to rewind and shoot Take II. Some obvious examples for shooting Take II:

- The scene is about Joe, but a player calls him "Biff."
- continuity is broken; we're led to expect a confrontation, but it never happens.
- The image is shaky or out of focus.
- One player thinks the scene is about making money, while the other thinks it's about sports.
- Players contradict each other.
- Visual—there's a hot spot, a silhouette that doesn't work or bad framing.
- Audio—a voice is weak, you can't make sense of a conversation, or noise interfering—traffic, another conversation, a fire engine, a hum.

Before shooting Take II, make one little change in Coach's Signal, activity, or emotion. That will help make Take II fresh. Take III? That depends on schedule: how much time can you spend on one scene?

Where to Cut Action

Here are the easiest places to tap the Camera Operator on the shoulder and cut:

- at a strong line, or a loud line
- at the end of a fade (a fade indicates time is passing or the location is changing)
- at the end of an activity, for example when a fish is caught
- at the end of an action: a woman, for instance, hands in her resignation
- when the volume and excitement of players hits a peak (or stops dead)

⌘ Matching Coach's Signal to improv scene

Choose the Coach's Signal you'd use for each of these scenes.

1) 2 campers say goodbye to each other.   _____
2) 3 office workers try to fix the copy machine.   _____
3) A woman has to tell her friend that a mutual friend has died. _____
4) A driver appeals to a judge to waive his speeding ticket   _____
5) 4 senior citizens in a center check out a new nurse   _____
6) A college freshman bets a senior that the Jets will win   _____
7) A father tells his daughter that he doesn't have her college tuition _____
8) A salesman gives a customer a high price on a 1988 Toyota.   _____

Here are suggested answers for matching the improv with Coach's Signal above:

1) campers—5-Second Delay
2) copy machine—Slo/Mo-Fast/Mo
3) death of a friend—Mood Swing
4) drive—Status Switch
5) senior citizens—Three Words + Contact
6) bet—Overlap

7) tuition—Mood Swing + Contact
8) car sale—make contact with the car

Is Something Happening?

Think of each improv as a *process*—not a win-lose decision or climax. They say the soul of stage drama is conflict, but that's not necessarily true of improv. Look at this scene.

A woman asks her husband to fix the toilet. He repairs the wire to the float, but the toilet now overflows. He takes off the lid, which falls and chips. When he rushes to get a mop, he turns abruptly and the handle hits his wife on the head. She gets up, fixes the toilet, and then goes back to her work. Quite a lot *happens* in that scene, but there is no *fight*.

What makes life so interesting is that we never know how things are going to come out. A player who doesn't know how a scene will end is more alert, more interested, more open than a player who does know. Your job is to keep the end of a scene open to many possibilities. For instance, when the boss calls you into his office, you don't know whether you'll be complimented, fired, or given more work to do.

Even if you know, for instance, that a scenario calls for you to break up with your friend, you do *not* know whether it will happen curtly or angrily, calmly or stonily. These are quite different roads to the same ending, and more than one of them should be available to you. Suppose the scenario calls for this:

Scene 1: Pam's company is sold and moves to Denver.

Scene 2: Pam and her husband go home to pack.

It's not *packing* that's important but *how* Pam packs and *how* her husband packs that shows how he feels about moving to Denver. In the same way:

Scene 1: Al invites his coworker, Nora, to a home-cooked meal.

Scene 2: The meal, which is not as important as *how* it's cooked.

For instance maybe Nora has a glass of wine and goes crazy over Al's Tiffany lamp, then cleans greasy burners, steams a dry artichoke, sings early Madonna. While he pounds sliced onion into hamburger meat and boils beets into a cream sauce that his last girlfriend taught him. The process is them—*feeling each other out*. Whether Nora spends the night on his couch is not the point. Whether she decides to take the #9 subway at 2 a.m. is not the point.

There is no fight. The scene is how they read each other—and how first impressions influence whether they reach out to each other again.

Think of each scene as 100 sparks flowing in time over 2 or 3 minutes. Encourage players to lock onto each other—physically and emotionally. When one moves, the others have an impulse to move. When one expresses emotion, the others have the impulse to express whatever they are feeling—fully. Pay attention to what players are doing, saying, and not quite expressing (i.e., impulses).

√ Checklist for coaches

Imagine you're shooting a scene in which a couple decides at 2 a.m. who's going to stay up with their sick baby. Here are elements for an improv; all of them can be changed—by you.

scenario—What could happen? What must happen—according to the scenario?

location—How could the location be enriched? How long would that take?

characters—Are they believable, consistent, interesting? Is it too late to make a cast change? Would the player object?

props/costumes—What will make characters interesting?

activity—Will it be toothpick, mosquito, or newscast that gives the player focus?

feeling—Are they ready to express it? Can they?

lighting—Should the Camera Operator move it, amplify it, reduce it?

sound—Has the Camera Operator checked for the noise of an air conditioner or fan? Does the scene need a boombox radio or music? Who will make the sound of the sick baby, of the party going on upstairs?

Coach's Signal—Do you need one? Which one? How will you remove it once it's done what you want?

Advice for a Coach

Build on the impulses. They are what is least contrived (i.e., "thought out").

Be positive and very encouraging.

When something is awful, ask players to "make another choice."

Draw out what's in the player with minimal "direction." Only if the player is stuck, go in with suggestions.

Have fun. It's only life!

Diane Mandle,
Project Manager & Coach

Bottom line: after every take, check the video you shot. Make sure the image is clean and the sound clear before going on to the next take.

If you have strong players, most of these elements fall right into place. The elements I forget are hats and props. Your movie is always better if players remember to wear a hat & carry a prop, which tells us a little bit about who they are.

Let's get it right: improv is a great tool, however, your apartment house is not built through improv, nor is your appendix removed by improv.

Vic Teich
LTV PAPA, Ex-President

Figure 31. Bob Bregman, Host of the Thanksgiving video holiday 1991, is convinced he is Squanto—savior of the Puritan Colony. The feather just says, "Somebody is aware Squanto must have a feather, so here it is." Granny glasses, one yellow glove or a plastic crutch also speak loudly to the viewer about a player in character.

13 Camera Operator in the Field

Who'll carry the tripod? Even in our age of handheld camerawork, a tripod can make the difference between a so-so shot and an excellent one.

It's such a relief, after the bustle of improv footage, to see a rock-steady shot of a distant tree—with maybe a hint of music. The viewer needs an escape from plot, a moment to appreciate and digest what's happened. The viewer needs to experience, for a minute, nothing. And distance, best captured on a tripod, can give you that *nothing*.

The viewer also needs to glimpse the panorama behind action—whether honeybees lowering themselves onto petals, hands busily arranging a buffet or rare books in a posh antique store. You want to read a few titles? With a tripod you can! One steady pan allows you to savor details of the culture that the action passed over.

Why not let players move in and out of a fixed frame—at will? When motionless the camera gives a sense of our being totally present—not chasing after headshots. As soon as one frame becomes familiar, cut, shift the tripod, angle the camera, and shoot again. For example, first we might see legs and boots swishing through the frame, then hands and beer steins rising to a tap, then dart players hunching in and out as they squint at a dartboard.

No tripod? You can make a makeshift one out of your body. Flatten it against a wall, tree, or a lamppost, and shoot handheld with confidence.

Figure 32. Teamwork, "Get Used to It" (1999), Nancy Fletcher, Mike Sehena, Dan Damato.

Shooting a movie makes you more aware of what's around you: buildings you've ignored forever, conversations you've never paid attention to. You start filming the world with your eyes. Every frame is a candidate for your movie.

Elisa Abatsis
Production Assistant

√ Checklist before leaving for the shoot

- **batteries**—Charged? How long will they give power if I use manual focus, if I use automatic focus? How many minutes will it take to recharge them? Is a 110-volt outlet available?
- **extension cords**—Have they been packed? 3-to-2 adaptors? Reflector board? Mic & boom? Music cassettes & boombox?
- **tripod**—Working smoothly? Will I need help to move the tripod up so I can shoot down? Am I relaxed enough to shoot handheld?
- **microphones**—When I need an external mic, who will hold it?
- **labels**—Will I start the tape by shooting a graphic of the title, or recording audio over an establishing shot? Or will I wait until I can edit in the studio or on a computer?
- **the Coach**—How will he or she signal me—so neither the countdown nor the word, "Cut," is heard on the tape?
- **rhythm**—Do I want my footage to look brisk or slow (a shot every 3 seconds, or every minute)?
- **lens & filter**—Use a wide angle lens? Which filter?
- **style**—Should I focus meticulously on the clothes and bodies of players? Should I raise the volume of the boombox and ask players to turn up their body language? Or go for reaction shots with minimum dialog and no music? Or wheel around the players to get fluid footage?

Camera Operators have as many ways to improvise as players do!

Recording Take II

This is a basic skill—to insure all takes are good and to give us instant replay after the shoot. *Editing in camera* is the visual discipline on which our program depends. Your camcorder's ability to erase a take depends on its counter. Some camcorders offer a zero memory function, by which you press a button and command the camcorder to return to zero. Reset the counter to zero at the beginning of every scene. At the end of the scene, let the tape run for about 2 seconds. If your Coach wants to reshoot, simply rewind to zero and play to a STOP point. Practice rewinding quickly and accurately.

You Can't Pause Forever

VHS Camcorder Operators: you need to know how many seconds your camcorder stays in PAUSE. Beyond that time it will automatically switch to STOP. Then you'll have to PLAY, SCAN backwards, PLAY forward until you see the frame where you want to begin and PAUSE there.

Dropout

Depending on the quality of the tape, if you RECORD more than 3 to 4 times on the same tape, you may get *dropout*—those distorting squares of color that show some of the emulsion on the tape has been worn away through repeated use.

Let Participants Shoot

Picking up a camcorder, focusing, and shooting are thrills a participant can get—along with playing and coaching. How do you satisfy the individual without risking the quality of the main tape—when you have only one camera?

Figure 33. Youthful participant shoots warm- up for Boy Meets Girl theme (2003). Photo credit: Claudia Gere.

Use two tapes. Label them #1 Story and #2 Documentation. Before, during and after the shoot, pop the Story tape out of your camcorder and put the documentation tape in. Ask participants to shoot Brainstorm or Warm-Ups, for instance.

If you don't have time, ask the Project Manager or Experience Host to show guests how to capture:

- a location on the Locations tape
- a few players on the Screen Test tape
- reactions by participants to the program
- warm-ups in character before the shoot
- warm-ups in the middle of the shoot
- any off-camera meetings, excitement, horseplay, intimacy, argument...
- the cast watching the screening and getting prizes

Remember always to switch tapes when you go back to shooting the story. Because players are more at ease off camera, don't be surprised if the documentation tape has more vitality than the Story tape.

If you walk away from a take without turning off the camera, letting it dangle from you arm, you'll get some very interesting feetage.

Kevin Gray

Modes

I know 5 ways to put a movie together.

Linear

Each scene triggers the next scene. And the last scene offers an end to the story.

How to Tell If You're In...

Create a portrait of a community. What makes Smithburg Smithburg is the question, and the answer is in the mouths of well-known bartenders, politicians, and street people. Improv scenes reflect issues.

Team Play

Gather people of one age in one location, another age in another location nearby. Let each team interact naturally around personal concerns. At each location a Coach is ready to call for the Camera to come shoot what's happening. The scenario calls for all teams to meet at a location where they find a resolution.

Thematic

Give the cast the job of finding improvs having to do with one theme. Between scenes cut to a commentator or to a series of very short images (called default footage).

The Camera Writes the Movie

The Players take the direction of the camera and find purely visual ways to express the relationships between them. The following short warm-up stimulates teamwork in the cast and develops intuition.

    Camera writes the movie

The players use guesswork since the camera doesn't talk. When it moves to a staircase, for instance, players go downstairs in front of it. When it heads outdoors, players are there—in activity.

The camera shoots from inside their group. When it does a 2-shot, 2 people start playing. When it focuses on a prop, someone picks it up and uses it. When it focuses on the sky, we hear a monolog.

Make up your own rules. There is no scenario because the camera is "writing" it moment to moment. Don't worry about making sense. Just play for the camera.

Use the Close/Far Coach's Signal with players who have soft voices and muted gestures.

14 Scenarios in the Field

Here are 10 spines on which to build a scenario. They were written long before they were produced. Some have been shot more than once. May they be useful to you if players cancel the big shoot because of bad weather or family.

Spine: With great difficulty you throw something out; you're glad it's gone, but it keeps coming back. This idea is so basic it triggers many familiar stories about former friends coming back, diseases that were cured once and for all, pets that were given away, paintings that were sold, discarded habits, old debts, bad loans, dangerous procedures, unwanted antiques, ex-spouses.

Example: "Boomerang Kids." A mature couple plan to move to the Southwest when their three children (all in their thirties) show up on the doorstep. Each has a different, compelling emergency. The parents listen sympathetically, but late that night they stick a note on the fridge to say they've left: "Work it out on your own." They do.

Spine: A dream gives you advice, which sends you to friend after friend for more advice, which you decide to take (or reject). It turns out to be bad (or good) advice.

Example: "The Dream of the Pharaoh," interpreted by Joseph, about 7 fat years and 7 lean years was good advice and saved Egypt.

Spine: You lose everything, but by believing that you're a superior human being, you find your niche.

Example: "Shanty Queen" by Lutzer, Harding, & Shepherd. A PhD candidate who's lost her family's support gets thrown out onto the street for not paying her rent. She never loses her towering superiority and survives threats of assault and despair to become a celebrity and key protestor for rights of the homeless.

Spine: You look everywhere for something you desperately need and find it's been right next door waiting for you the whole time (True Story.)

Example: "The 167ᵗʰ Date." A widower advertises to find a mate and goes on 166 dates in several cities. Finally he responds to an unusual ad from a woman. She lives next door. Their apartments are exactly alike. So are their personalities. The two lonely people find each other to be totally compatible.

Spine: A parent has so much trouble raising children and is so critical of them that she/he finally gets rid of them.

Example: "Minister's Daughter" by David Shepherd. A politically active minister renounces his children, claiming the son is too conservative, the daughter too wild. When he informs them they are adopted, the daughter bolts, gets in big trouble with a dope dealer. The son takes over as father and bails his sister out of jail. They drive off in a rented car to share their new understanding of who they are.

Spine: A teacher is so brilliant that his prize students appropriate his techniques and set up classes without him; he loses his only job.

Example: "Art of Failure" by E. J. Palven. An Italian professor joins a learning network to teach the art of failure. One of his students is a paranoid dying for affection; one is an activist who's denied himself a girlfriend till his candidate wins; one is a grandmother trying to cast away her family. He helps them so successfully that he offers an advanced seminar, but he too now fails: one of his students has stolen the idea of his course and has arranged to teach it.

Spine: With great authority people predict calamity; when it doesn't happen, they are unhappy.

Spine: Rural teenagers start a project that's mocked by parents, siblings, and neighbors. But their club gets the right licenses and buys the right food and drink. It's such a big success that Starbucks makes them an offer to buy them out. "Teen Café" by Stephanie Carlson.

Spine: Several people are persuaded they're not living fully and should get professional help. They go for training and are transformed, but when they get home, they alienate the very people they wanted to get closer to. "The Real You" by Elaine May.

Spine: A woman travels to a fashionable resort to attend a posh fundraiser but loses her purse en route and is turned away at the door. Running out of gas in the dark, she staggers through brambles to a friendly group that lives on the "wrong side of the tracks." They welcome her, feed her, gas up her car, and send her home. "Rest of the Hamptons" by Denise Mourges.

16 Pre-Production Spines

Spine: An envious woman notices her girlfriends take big risks that pay off—whether in romance or on the stock market. She copies them in every detail but misses the fine points. She's losing a fortune in friends and money when she halts and decides to stop grasping at life and instead start living it.

Spine: Party Story—deciding who to invite, preparations, first guests, the big shots, playing games, dancing, goofing, sly romancing, giant arguments, the first to leave, those who stay and stay and stay, cleaning up the mess while talking about what happened, the last candle is blown out.

Spine: Searching out a special recipe, tracking down ingredients, getting advice from experts, complex preparations, too many cooks? It's a triumph (or a flop) that's shared with family and neighbors while the whole story is told again and again.

Spine: Two siblings are separated at birth when their mother gives them up for adoption. Years later she tracks them down excitedly, phones them. They're dying to meet her. One finds she's an interesting person while the other does not. He rejects her just as she once rejected him.

Spine: A 13-year-old boy finds Cadillac with keys in ignition. He starts it up & drives around town, showing off and taking friends for rides. After several close calls with police and other adults, he returns car to where it was parked, sits nearby. Owner & family members walk up. Boy gives them key and a tall story about how he saved their car from the Mafia.

Spine: Scenes in a moving car, traveling from home to store to office: Son & Mother, Mother & Father, Father & Friend, etc. All of them are worried about Charlie. We get many ideas of who Charlie is—until we meet him in last scene.

Spine: People lifting weights, doing push-ups, jogging while working on a problem; they agree, disagree, go get advice. We see man & wife, then man & daughter, man & business advisor, wife & friend—until an entire society comes into view and the problem disappears.

Spine: In a crisis, it's a woman (or girl) who outshines a man (or boy). He pretends he's the strongest and can't face the fact that he's dependent on a female. She encourages his self-deception.

Spine: A poor relative comes to live with a rich family. One by one he converts them to beliefs, which give the exact strength & peace each of them needs. One day he's gone.

Spine: If people around you are not having a good time, you blame yourself. You set out to remove their complaints—one after another. You realize some will be dissatisfied no matter what. But you work on them until you give up. Then you rest—, satisfied. Dissatisfied?

Spine: For years you work for something hard to get. You strategize and exaggerate and crawl and assert your right to get it. When you finally do, you find it's a total disappointment, for example, an honorary title.

Spine: Parents warn kids about a terrible influence that they pinpoint and resist. But this same influence is attractive to one kid, who confronts it, embraces it, tames it, and leaves home with it in his or her pocket.

Spine: A parent is constantly critical of her young son until she gets very sick. He proves to be the only one who can care for her. He does so and finds he's becoming as critical as his mother was, while daily, Mom turns into a child.

Spine: Two compulsive friends bet each other on the movement of stocks, of birds, of rain clouds—it doesn't matter. They start betting on whether friends will stay single, marry, or separate. When they bet a lot of money on whether they'll lose their jobs, the one who is fired wins the bet. They decide to give up betting for the sake of their friendship.

Spine: A woman goes bankrupt, much to the horror and shame of her parents, who advise her how to pay off the debt. But she uses the experience as a step to a bigger venture with wealthy partners. She proclaims to family and friends, "Bankruptcy is just a short course on economics."

Developing Surprise

Surprise is the hallmark of improv, not comedy or conflict: will the retiring worker lose a $45,000 pension, or not? How will the teenager spend his Christmas money—on hip-hop or lab kit? Will the woman propose to the man, or vice versa? Who will win the fight—the scrawny little guy or the sumo wrestler? You write it.

⌘ Invent a surprise for these locations

driving through the Okefenokee swamps

adopting twin girls from Afghanistan

opening a package in orange plastic from New Mexico

sitting down to chitchat with your new mother-in-law

joining an inner-city hospital as a woman intern

coming home for your 16th birthday party, your 21st, 30th

Since none of us can plan out the future, our stories have to be riddled with surprise to be real. We need not vampires, clowns or extraterrestrials, but characters in focus and full of feeling who surprise us!

7 Beginnings and Ends

In the field you may have to invent a scenario on the spot. If your main player is late, do you quit? No, just fill in the middle of one of these frameworks. Invent scenes for the middle depending on how many players you have and what the point of the story is.

Spine beginning: A woman leaves her first husband because of his bad behavior and goes looking for an entirely different man...**invent a middle**...Her second husband looks different from the first but turns out to have the same behavior. **End.**

Spine: A girl drives to NYC, parks next to Tompkins Square and steps into a sea of homeless people...**invent a middle**...Days later, when her distraught mother finds her, she says she had fun and plans to do it again (True Story).

Spine: A woman invites her best friend to work together on a commercial project...**invent a middle**...When her friend gets control, she boots her out, but the client finds out what happened and the friend is fired.

Spine: A retiring leader chooses the weakest person he can find to take over...**invent a middle**...The replacement proves to be realistic, smart, and tenacious.

Spine: A couple can't get their 25-year-old son to move out, find a job, and become self-sufficient...**invent a middle**...He lands a job with foreigners & sends home a tombstone as a present for his parent's anniversary.

Spine: At work a supervisor refuses a promotion, but it's given to him any way...**invent a middle**...When he becomes president, he's asked what his secret is. He claims his rise is all a mistake: he had nothing to do with any part of it.

Spine: Fed up with his intimate friends, his job & home, a man cuts loose...**invent a middle**...In a new city years later, we see him with the same kinds of friends, working the same kind of job, and living in the same kind of home with the same kind of woman.

A speedy approach: take a theme that interests the group, Brainstorm scene ideas, cast, and shoot; for instance,

- "Guilt of the Parents"
- "Partings and Meetings"
- "Making It Big."

Figure 34. Legend leads comfortably to video storytelling. Here the stupid brother, Tim Holcum, fails to kill his wimpy brother, Tim Van Ness.

First Scenario Produced in Chicago COMPASS

In "Game of Hurt" by Paul Sills, 1954, a cigar salesman and his wife pass the time by playing a game of insults. At the local bar he gets so fed up with her pretension he sells her to a steel-working country boy. After a night of hot Southern compliments, she comes home because she misses the insults.

"2 Families" by Pat Mew and David Shepherd

Here's how a 2-sentence idea can generate 16 scenes. Improvs will run an average of 2 minutes each. Format is Team Play with 3 locations: dysfunctional family, the childless couple, cops.

Location 1: Stacie's family, Saturday morning: coffee & beer. Dad and Mom argue about how to control Stacie, who's been out all night. Stacie shows up, speaking to brother Clem but to neither parent. Parents smack her. Will they send her to Granny, who's strict?

Location 2: Cocktail party & fundraiser at home of childless couple; they point out famine areas on a globe. Will guests donate?

Location 3: Outside grocery, two cops study poster that says, "Want to be adopted? Call this number." Will they rip it down?

Location 2: Couple quiz each other on problems that will arise in adoption; where to put child's bed and what about prayer, privacy, discipline? What are their answers?

Location 1: In bathroom Mom prays to God, blaming herself for Stacie's behavior. Is she forgiven?

Location 2: Stacie shows up at door of Couple, with their poster. When Couple asks questions she nods yes or no, negotiating terms of her adoption. Will she stay?

Location 1: Granny's kitchen with lurid family drama on TV. Granny & Mom recall Mom's pranks as a child. Is Granny willing to take Stacie in?

Location 3: On street, cops use cell phone to call the telephone number on poster.

Location 2: Husband answers phone, says adoption has taken place successfully. Wife is getting Stacie into elaborate bedtime ritual, including prayer. Will Stacie go along with it?

Location 1: Midnight. Dad comes home with buddies. Clem tells him what Dad's done wrong, why Stacie has split. Buddies stick up for Dad? Will Dad defend himself?

Location 2: Morning with neighbor kids: Stacie plays tough, shows off at touch football. Will kids accept her authority?

Location 1: Dad asks cops into his kitchen to report Stacie missing. Can she be found?

Location 2: Stacie complains to Couple about abuse she has suffered from her parents. Stories escalate. Will the Couple believe them?

Location 3: Cops show up at home of Couple, who say they are simply protecting Stacie from abuse. She refuses to leave. How do Cops make her leave?

Location 1: Granny answers door as Cops return Stacie. Granny says she won't take Stacie in unless Stacie speaks. Does Stacie speak? If so, what does she say?

Location 2: Couple celebrates end of ordeal—no court citations, no bones broken, no house burned down. Dad and Mom burst in screaming and threaten couple with all the above.

"The August" by Deb Lacusta

In this scenario, done in Chicago and New York City in 1982, a Guru and his Trainer are invited to town by a disgruntled, negative cult. The Guru manages to get their confidence and offers them properly cynical advice along with rituals of his faith.

Midsummer, the Guru announces he's had a vision: The world will end on August 1. His followers are appalled; what are they to do until the day of reckoning? The Guru listens to his follower's questions, gives answers, and accepts gifts and money, which he hands on to his Trainer.

In this section individual players choose what each will do:

- break the law
- ignore sexual liaisons
- run up huge credit card debt
- steal
- attack enemies

August 1st arrives, and the world doesn't disappear. The Guru's followers are rabid. He explains the meaning of what has happened. They withdraw in a funk.

The Trainer reviews the time his Guru spent—what he did right and what he did wrong. The two of them have been booked into San Diego. They plan how to make a greater monetary success of their next venture.

Six to 8 players can easily bring off the story. It's an excuse to try out new players in crowd scenes. It's also an opportunity for every player to freely shape a scene that grows out of the certainty that he or she will die soon.

Except for the last scene, the plot flows with no interruption toward August 1. The last scene is shocking and puts the whole story into a new light. If you have extra players, they can play neighbors who relate to the cultists with amusement or pity.

Storyboards remind us of the story & show how bodies & shapes relate in the frame. They should show how the scene is to be shot. Use stick figures only.

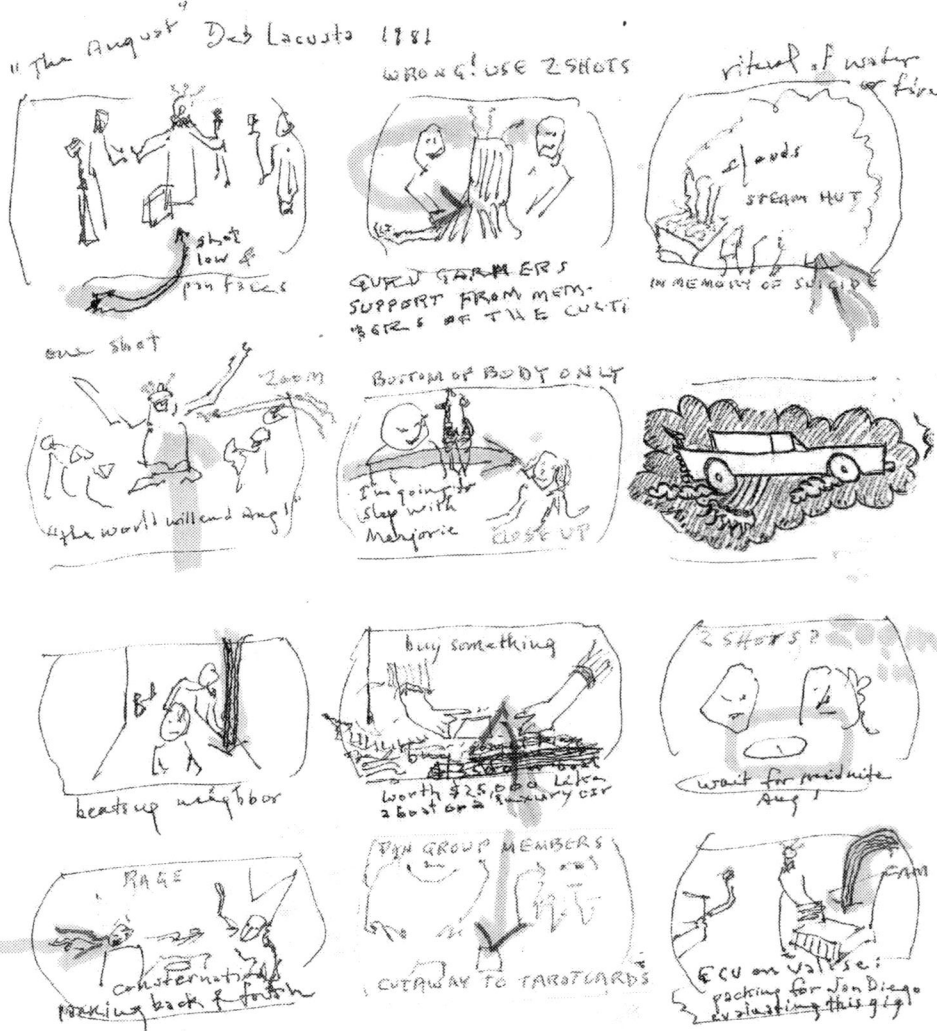

Figure 35. Storyboard for "The August" by Deb Lacusta (1981).

The drawing of the car is by a professional artist, Chase Carlyle. Is his figure at the back of the car the thief? How will the scene be shot? How will the thief break in?

"Seven Portals to Paradise" by Roget & Shepherd

This scenario was dictated by Tiffany Roget to David Shepherd 5/97 in Chicago, transcribed 7/97 on the QE2, and sent to Tiffany c/o Second City.

Monolog by Tiffany over trucking shots of middle-class homes (like opening of "Down by Law"). "One day I realized I'd done everything I could for myself. I'd outgrown my upbringing."

Basement. Father moving cabinet downstairs while quarreling with Mother. He turns to Tiffany and says, "These are the concerns of adults. Get out." (Person playing Tiffany should play younger than her age.)

Dance studio. Tiffany & 4 women do fast physical exercises, silently. The teacher lectures them on their obligation to be happy. The music is "Shake your Booty" by Triptotronix.

Bar. 5 guys discuss sexy chicks & in particular Tiffany. When she appears, they pounce on her, literally. One gets her to give him her phone number. Michael steals it from him.

Kitchen. Michael's parents stack up dirty dishes for him to wash. He announces he's leaving—for Canada. They mock him, predict he'll catch sexual disease and chronic unemployment.

Old car. 5 guys pack Michael's car to overflowing. When Michael carries up more boxes to be packed, they tease him. A dog runs on; they pack the dog.

On the highway. The dog craps under Tiffany. Michael and Tiffany do not waver from happiness. In Chicago the motor conks out.

Chicago, single room. They inspect and rent a tattered room from a dour landlady. It has no furniture except a bed. What brings them joy? The dog.

Dawn in one room. Michael enters from jogging. With dog he meditates. Tiffany sleeps.

Studio. Tiffany in acting class with 6 students. They play Freeze Tag, then Freeze Tag with Characterization. One after another students tag Tiffany's partner: "You had to be a big shot, di'n't you?" "You had to open up your mouth." "You had to be a big shot, di'n't you?" "Your friends were all knocked out." Tiffany squeals with excitement.

Subway platform. The 6 keep the same characterizations, play the same game. Michael joins them, plays. Subway passengers look on as if watching monkeys.

Mick's class. Students are listless: Mick explodes, "F**k this, f**k that! Get out there and do something! Count money. You're at McDonald's counting people...Faster, faster. You're counting French fries." Generate maximum physical activity.

Single room. Michael comes home to Tiffany as she meditates with the dog. He kisses her on the top of her head.

Studio. Tiffany in Gelman's class. She's discovering why she thinks what she thinks, liberating herself to live life in the moment. Gelman says, "Be where you're at when you're there. Experience life to the extent you think you should" (that is, turn life off and on).

Park. Michael approaches Tiffany meditating while upright. He kisses her on the head while goosing her. She turns slowly; it's not Tiffany. Is he humiliated? Not at all: he describes her energy to her, which he says thrills him.

Stage. Rehearsal for comedy show. Michael & Tiffany laugh hysterically. "Isn't it wonderful," they say at intermission. "Any time we want, we can come here and get so much joy in just two hours of living life."

Park. On way home they make up a game: "Give me 60 seconds of Joy/Joy." Each has to sing or dance—or reveal him or herself verbally. Treat this as a variety show. When players lose steam it's the end of the scenario.

"Man Who Went Looking for Death,"
African Folktale

There once was a man so down on his luck he went around beating up tough guys to get himself killed. On the street he met Death's Messenger and begged him, "Take me." The Messenger said it wasn't the right time and gave him some money.

The man bet all of it on a game of dice and won! He walked into a business and demanded a job; it was his. A woman who was watching offered to put him up. Soon, to celebrate their love, they threw a party.

Death showed. The man said "I'm doing so well; thanks for the money. I'm happy. Why are you here?" "Because," said Death, "I have time for you today."

"Septembersong" by David Shepherd

This is the story of an old woman, who's trying to get her children to pay for heart surgery for her husband. He dies in some pain.

The children come to the funeral. It's cold. They feel he lived his quota. They each speak about him. The old woman collapses from an attack of cold.

She goes home, tries to live. One day, she sees some kids getting rid of a vagrant in their park. She shoos them off and talks to the man in his language—Greek. He's very sweet, good-looking, and lost. She lets him sleep in her hallway. The kids tell their parents about the woman taking in the immigrant.

She treats him to a shower. What can he do for her? He asks. "Hug me." she answers. She warms up. She lives again.

The police visit to find out why the vagrant is staying with the old woman. She explains in terms of his need. They explain, "Him and his buddies are not wanted." They advise her to get rid of him.

Middle of the story. See Bertolt Brecht story: "The Old Woman."

He becomes completely dependent on her for advice; where to find work, how to make the most of his visa, where to get free clothing, how to buy cheap food. All of which he repays by hugging her whenever she feels cold. They are indelibly attached.

End of story: he comes home from a job painting. He panics, knowing she is in a big house where a party is going on. He goes from room to room without finding her. In one room the radicals welcome him and ask questions about his country's politics (with Bill Dwight). In another, guests in masks are dancing. In another, kids draw him into their game. Each room is a trap. He still can't find her.

She is on the beach, which is frosty. She comes to a lighted figure on the dunes. She sits in front of it. She's dying. Her man runs across the sand. The figure on the dunes says heaven is grateful for her. Heaven is ready for her. Her man is running. She is ready for heaven.

"I'm Getting 7 Million Dollars" by Izzy Gesell

A number of people, who don't know each other (or even of each other's existence) have received an invitation to attend the reading of the will of one Jane Campbell, an extremely wealthy and eccentric woman.

Enclosed with the invitation is a round-trip ticket and travel directions to Ms. Campbell's home. A spouse, lover, or child is also invited.

Each invitee has a different recollection of who Campbell was and how they got connected. This becomes evident as the parties arrive and are told they will have to spend a weekend at the Campbell site before the will is read. The entire fortune will go to just *one* of the attendees.

They also are told they will be judged during the weekend but no one knows who the judges are or even what they're being judged on.

As the invitees mill around, mingle and talk to each other and among themselves, it's clear Campbell was a different person to each of them. It's also clear the promise of big money affects each of them.

Specifics

- One character seduces another because she thinks he's the judge.
- Children see through all adult bull****.
- Wheeler-Dealer tries to sell a financial service to everybody there.
- Married couple splits over what to do with the money if they win.

15 Fourteen Case Studies

Here are high points and low points in the development of MOVIExperience from Day One.

The First MOVIExperience

It was in the sub-basement of Tribeca Lab, sponsored by that impresario of the bizarre and beautiful—Al Ramos. Having never actually done my new format, I didn't know the best way to get into it. We were sitting around the stage, staring at leftovers of past shows piled on top of each other —junk, fabric, furniture.

"What's the theme of the show we're about to do?" I asked.

Everyone gave a 1-word theme: *guilt, submission, love,* etc.

"Vote for the theme you like best."

Deception was the winner. But where was the first scene to be shot? I asked the cast to look at the stage junk and give it a name or place. They decided it was either:

- the home of a recently deceased man,
- a junk shop,
- an antique store, or
- the office of a theatrical agent.

The last suggestion appealed to everyone. "This agent is a woman," Marlene explained, "and that's her casting couch" (where the agent tests the actor's attraction to her). The story was now seeded.

Players came and went, but a basic cast stayed. I pushed our unlikely premise through five locations. Different women playing the Agent gave sharply different motivations. Whenever we got lost, one of the players, Jack Murphy, came up with a legal or psychological explanation for what we were doing. We searched for an ending and found it.

After 4 hours we piled into two taxis and took our cassette to my apartment for a premiere screening of a premiere format—toasted with red wine from David Haber.

Doubling Roles

When players who've committed don't show up and don't phone, what do you do?

- Reschedule the shoot for another day?
- Run a tiny workshop?
- Give up and go home?
- Phone the people who promised to come?
- Shoot whatever asks to be shot?

The following shows what 4 players can do.

Ellen, Stephanie, Trevor, and I saw there was work to do on a scenario by my ex-student, Michael Golding. It's about a boy who's so infatuated with a recurring dream girl, that he's become a Dream Slave.

We asked: how would she appear?—through the window? No, we decided; she comes from under the sheets.

Should we use gauze over the lens to suggest she's a fantasy? No, she should look real. What's unreal about her is her relationship to Trevor; the viewer has to get that.

Well, does Stephanie play Dream Girl like a fairy or an angel? No, she just treats Trevor, who's 15, as if he were a man-god.

OK, who plays the Real Girl? Stephanie herself; she is Dream & Reality at once. Ellen is Sister & Mother at once. As for me, I'll be Trevor's Dead Dad and also his Therapist.

With costume changes, the revised scenario took us two hours to shoot; it runs 6 scenes. "Who shot?" you may wonder. Trevor, our Dream Slave. The camera is the player. The audience hears his voice, and when he gets scolded, his camera drifts out onto the woods or up onto the ceiling. Every frame is seen from his ravenous, love-sick point-of-view.

This was our best video of the month because it was dense, unpredictable, vivid, puzzling. The action slips from dream to reality more than once in the same scene, for instance, in Trevor's appointment with a Barefoot Therapist or the Murder of his Dream Girl by his fiancée. With Stephanie in two costumes, we shot in reverse: first from the position of the Dream Girl, then from the Real Girl.

Suppose a dozen players had shown up. Could we have achieved such intimate meaning, surprise doubling or tight teamwork? The doubling which gives the piece its individuality would never have been necessary.

Choosing the Right Signal

When a high-tech telecommunications company asked to do a MOVIExperience, we anticipated no one on their staff had improv training. The scenario they developed was stuffed with deception and violence, which can look awkward & unlikely on tape—even when enacted by professionals.

We knew we'd have to use Coach's Signals. But which ones?

The weakest scene was a pallid confrontation between father & step-daughter. Its location was vague; somewhere between swimming pool and house. Having been slipped in at the last minute, the scene had no muscle.

I decided to use 5-Second Delay. This signal freezes players in the rush of words:

The stammering stepfather makes one jerky appeal after another to the girl, who considers each one and quashes it. Delays get longer and more painful:

... "Your mother and I—we both care for you. Look! You're smoking!" Delay... as she lights up

"Nobody really cares if I do or not." Delay...as she puffs.

"I care! How do you think I feel about kids smoking?" DELAY as she turns.

"I think you should go care about somebody else." Delay...

Slow pans from face to face show weathered shingles behind the players; there is no activity except the offending king-size cigarette. But the scene is surprisingly solid because the Coach's Signal is right. The viewer says, "This relationship is so bad it can only get better." And it does improve—later.

Continuity & Pacing

A constant danger in improv is speeding. The Coach thinks the scene is finished because he's achieved his goal, a change in the relationship. The Camera Operator gets tapped on the shoulder; the players hear "cut!" and stop. But when the tape is screened, it's skimpy. There's almost nothing there—no feeling, no activity, no movement to watch.

Before you leave a location, review the tape with an ear plug or headphones. Is the audio signal clear? How is the camera work? Do the players have any reality, that is, are they open to more than one ending? Do we care about them? Do they keep our interest? And finally, when recording stops, has something happened?

At "My Seven Million Dollars" players thought they were fulfilling Izzy Gesell's scenario. It had to do with the death of a woman whose house they were visiting—and her will, which was to be read. The most *correct* couple would get $7,000,000.

I thought the improvs were great until the screening. Then I saw: Too little action & too much conversation. The clusters of guests were motionless because they had no activities. They were afraid of being silent because they had little feeling for their dead friend. They forgot to search for a behavior that would show their character posturing for the prize of $7,000,000.

I should have kept them off camera till they discovered some feeling for their dead friend and for each other. Instead they all talked about how to spend $7,000,000, which only one guest will get. What an interesting situation! But it's not on the tape.

Sudden Cast Changes

Before a shoot I have a nightmare: the lead in a scenario will get a phone call halfway through the session, "Sorry, my baby has a fever. I have to go home."

It's too late to start from scratch, and there's no way to finish. You can't afford to refund fees. It seems the end of Improv World has arrived.

Well, this disaster has taken place already—in West New York at the home of Shirley & Jack Tannenbaum. We were shooting "Out of Bedlock" with engineers from Lucent—the story of a man and woman who get divorced but stay under the same roof because they can't afford separate apartments.

Twenty guests were two hours late. No Brainstorm was possible.

I convinced two systems analysts to start: play the wife and her new boyfriend. The camera tracks them from their car to her garage door, where she says haltingly: "I never do this, but would you like to come up for a coffee?"

Sometime later they are up five flights and stretched out on her bed. You may think that because they agreed to be intimate, I'm the Great Persuader. You're wrong: intimacy was no problem for them because they are married!

At this moment 20 more guests started to arrive. I picked a man to play the husband—a tall, loud business man, who wanted to know what jerk his former wife had brought into the apartment. He flung open her door; there was nobody in bed. The two systems analysts had disappeared. They didn't want to be in the movie any more. Catastrophe.

Two Black trainers took over their parts and without a hitch, finished the shoot. At the screening I was amazed. The guests loved the replacement of a tentative, soft spoken, white couple by a loud, brash, Black one. Twenty-five people were having an *experience* more delicious than screening a *movie*.

Many see improv as a new view of old friends. For instance, when I was shooting in a small room, a dozen friends squeezed in to watch their buddies—and whisper. When I asked them to leave so we could shoot without distraction, I realized they were as excited to be on location as to play a role.

Along with other disasters, unforeseen cast changes give just one more opportunity to create on your feet while making a movie.

Hindsight for Your Next Movie

In Northampton, we should have paid closer attention to the signs. We thought getting a lot of new customers would guarantee us success in our next shoot. We'd been comfortable playing with people from The Valley—an area of artistic innovation. Now we were getting city dwellers—from Springfield.

We were also getting a 4-year-old kid and a 7-year-old, whose mother told about their stunning living room performances. To hear the stories, we were lucky to get such prodigies.

But on camera with a scenario, these gifted children tended to freeze. They did exactly what they were asked to do, but there was no feeling. Their scenes were like a school exercise on which they scored "A" by reciting lines they made up before the shoot.

During the Brainstorm we invented three big scenes about our theme—leaving: leaving home, leaving marriage, and leaving a religion. The cast had to be split three ways and would have a lot of time to kill—since locations were far apart.

To occupy their time, our Documentation camera could have shot *other leavings* invented by players waiting to play their scene. The kids would have been fine doing a nonverbal scene—leaving a toy store, for instance. Other rich possibilities are leaving a job, sweetheart, poker game, church service, noisy tavern, pack of friends. Or leaving your life, your wits, your nasty habit, your last dollar—shot casually and quickly by the Project Manager and #2 Camera.

These contributions would come as a surprise when screened before the story tape. They'd give participants with time on their hands an unexpected entree into the creative process.

When the Cast Takes Over

"Don't worry about a thing."

"Just turn on the camera."

I was amazed: Earl and Michael had formulated, from my scanty remarks, a through line for Deb Lacusta's scenario, "The August," which they had not even read.

They knew how the guru would come to town, attract morbid followers, and deliver his announcement that the world will end on August 1. They were confident they could invent bizarre new behaviors for the cultists. And they saw the shape of the scene in which the followers confront their leader when the world doesn't end and everyone is still alive on August 2.

They even invented a scene missing from Deb's scenario: the Trainer criticizes the Guru for earning too little in rich New York. He expects a better performance (and a greater profit) in San Diego.

This scenario has a core of irony that makes it quick to grasp and easy to play. Such scenarios have an open-and-shut quality: every scene points to an end, and that end seems inevitable.

As for Earl & Michael, I can only say: their intuition is swift.

Brainstorm Inside a Brainstorm

Before shooting at Colrain, Massachusetts, Diane Mandle, our Project Manager, predicted what our theme would be. She'd seen the octagonal house where we'd be shooting, with all its tiny bedrooms and lofty platforms. She knew it was a perfect setting—for "Dreams."

For an hour at sunset the group trained—hard—on Diane's lawn. On her porch a picnic turned into a Brainstorm, but not one idea won group approval. Diane watched us struggle until she played her trump. All our skimpy ideas now became grist for her Dream Mill, where they transformed into viable scenes.

Indoors our group of 10 broke up into 3 mini-Brainstorms, each one in a different room. The energy of ideas kept rising. In 90 minutes we had more material than we needed.

It's unlikely that 10 people could each turn out one dream—working alone. And it's even less likely for our unwieldy group to turn out 10—working together.

A combination of very physical games, informal outdoor snacks, and cloistered groups seated on carpets brought reality to Diane's dream theme.

Using a Story Written in Advance

When you know you won't have much time to shoot, use a strong, existing story. You lose the intense creativity of the Brainstorm, but you make up for it in certainty—about roles and locations.

Make sure the story can be done in nearby locations by testing them in the light that you'll use. If the cast can't see itself in the story, either adapt the scenario to them or find more players.

Take Golding's "Backward Marriage." It's a straight tale of a bored couple; they play out romantic fantasies with other partners, inevitably get divorced. Nothing much here. The wife has a fetish about cleanliness, while the husband can't enjoy another woman romantically unless he's thinking about his wife. Somewhat blah—until you follow Golding's direction: play it backwards!

For our Research & Development sessions I needed a simple structure on which to test three methods of coaching:

- by using Coach's Signals,
- by having players take strong emotions, or
- by involving them in activities (such as shaving, cooking).

"Backward Marriage" was perfect! It was tight as a titanium drum. We added mother, mother-in-law, boyfriend, girlfriend. It still held up as it lurched jerkily into the past. In three versions the first scene shows the marriage in disarray at 7 a.m.; the last is the ecstatic couple rushing into the room where they'll spend their honeymoon.

Transformations in the relationship are marked by shocking jumps into the Before, Before, Before. Innocence is magically regained at the end while the viewer notices traits in each character that will one day break the marriage.

Gibberish in Improv

Gibberish is an improvised language that may sound Slavic, Latin, Asian, European... The words you make up are not nonsense; they have some meaning—at least for you. For instance, "fortiwa claban" might mean, "my shoes are killing me." Shoot players in an activity while they talk gibberish, and you can often guess from their expressions and gestures what they mean. Omar Shapli swears that one group of a dozen could, after speaking exclusively in gibberish for a week, tell what each other was saying.

We've shot whole videos in gibberish. A scene that worked was of a couple in a bathroom, where they were squeezing and sniffing pills. The woman was urging the man to try a pink one, and her excitement (in gibberish) was a perfect contrast to his reluctance.

Another scene was a commercial for hair spray—shot against a bank of flowers. On tape it appeared quite convincing—as if network TV were suddenly interrupted by a promo from Bosnia.

As you can guess, the reason teachers of improv use gibberish is to give players a reason to boost the physicality of their performance.

No Scenario

At the Harbor, an alternative high school in Altoona, Iowa, a dozen teens showed up for MOVIExperience. Nancy and I synopsized a dozen existing scenarios, all of them suitable, we thought, for this cast. No response.

Would the group agree to a Brainstorm—an intense activity requiring players to review options fast and vote on their favorite?

Nothing satisfactory came to the surface. Someone asked, "Why do we have to have a scenario?" We explained the scenario is traditional, it assures that you focus on what really interests you, it helps participants and camera get to the next location. That is, it speeds things up.

"Let's have no scenario," said Jane.

"Well, how will the camera know where to shoot?"

"Have arguments about interesting subjects and bury them in music from a boombox. Have people meeting or parting with no dialog. Just acid rock."

Nancy, who was uncomfortable with wide-open structures, suggested five threads to run through the piece: Argument, Frolic, The Chase, Family, and Future.

Because we had an empty amusement park to shoot in, her threads wove together neatly.

Rough action, sentiment, dispute, career, dating all threaded into the style that the teens were comfortable with. We found ourselves doing Iowa-style MTV.

A Life Scenario

At the MOVIExperience created by S. E. Polk High School, another Iowa school, 60 students choose a scenario by Izzy Gesell— "Tenth Class Reunion." Near Des Moines, I find these teens have overwhelmingly positive or negative notions about their future. In framing a scenario 10 years into the future, they add enough makeup to look 27, built a quirky relationship with a classmate, then flashed forward into affluence or failure.

We see one boy and girl refusing to speak to each other while in high school. Ten years later they are on opposite ends of a couch as a little boy wanders in with toy handcuffs. He cuffs his mother's hand to his father's. The two teens who once shunned each other are now parents.

The Queen of the class is, ten years later, still Queen—but of deceit. The girl who used to ignore the boy next door now gropes for a way to attract him since he's become a tycoon. Even teachers create a scene—playing poker at lunch while seething and fuming about work conditions.

It was a relief to have a scenario that everyone could add to. Scenes ranged from sci-fi to drama to slapstick, but the common starting point was a life that everyone in the cast knew cold—their own.

Personal Feelings Can Be Dangerous

At Pioneer Valley Performing Arts High School, I was given a long afternoon to lay out and shoot a video movie. The cast had been trained; the camera was in good hands.

We started the Brainstorm with a dozen students. Usually a dozen participants will bat themes back and forth for a couple of hours, relishing each other's ideas before voting on which to produce. But today there was little discussion. And when it came to a vote, almost everyone in the room chose self-destruction.

I felt as if my heart was being stroked with an icicle. "This is the wrong state to be in," I felt, "the wrong class to be teaching at, and the wrong cast for a video movie." When I made feeble objections, the group obliged me by switching to its second choice: obsession. I found this theme equally negative. But within an hour we had a scenario of some eight scenes—and a sure-fire player, Brian Marsh, Principal.

Scenes in the hallway, where shows are postered, had life. Shawn, a young obsessive, sneaks into a rehearsal where a resonant Brian is coaching Melinda.

By 5:30 they came together: cast, parents, schoolmates. I knew my personal feeling to their theme was faulty when I heard the audience cackle with laughter.

ACT NOW! a MOVIExperience Success Story

Nancy Fletcher has coached many MOVIExperiences with girls around the country. She founded ACT NOW! which uses the MOVIExperience format to build character and confidence in girls. Here are some thoughts and experiences—in her own words.

Authority

As coach you have to make decisions fast. I remember in Arizona, the players for the first scene arrived at its location before I did. By the time I got there, they had selected a place, figured out the scene, and practiced their lines. This went against what I had in mind, and it went against the spirit of improv. We don't practice a scene. We want dialogue fresh. As in life, there's nothing better than surprising someone with the unexpected. We want players to discover a scene, not predict it.

But I agreed to let them do the scene their way. They were thrilled! And did a great job. They laid the groundwork for a theme they wove throughout the movie. In the first scene Breanna told a joke but couldn't get the lines right. Her friends mocked her good-naturedly. She continued to try telling that joke and others throughout the movie. It wasn't until the girls staged their tenth high school reunion in the last scene when they decided that she should tell the joke—successfully this time. It made a perfect ending. The girls jumped out of their skins with triumph.

Positive Long-Term Effects

You only do what you can imagine yourself doing. So imagination comes first. Girls start out imagining the sky's the limit. Around 10 years old, their imaginations shrink, at least when it comes to what they believe they can do. Girls lower their sights and achieve less. Talent goes untapped. MOVIExperience widens their horizons; gives them role models of females doing what men do; gives them moving pictures of themselves taking action, shaping their story, taking charge.

I always hire female professionals to staff the MOVIExperience, and it is a female universe for the duration. The girls that are present fill all the roles that need filling. We expect them to do it. And, guess what? They do it—usually without batting an eye. Even though they sometimes admit being nervous.

There is sound scientific evidence that seeing repeated positive images of oneself is a very effective, inexpensive way to change behavior. So my hunch was right when I started ACT NOW! MOVIExperience is good for self-esteem, good for character, good for confidence. Nine months after one MOVIExperience event, a ten-year-old girl was discussing the movie with her director at Girls Inc., "People think Hollywood is so hard. But we can do it too. Just give us some money and equipment, and we can do it, too!"

A year later, one of the 12-year-olds in the same movie explained, "I didn't really know how I was inside. I didn't really care about that. The movie gave me a time to express myself. It showed me that a lot of people will like me if I express myself more." She now has many more friends.

Very shy Elizabeth Montmeny played the shy girl in a scene. At the screening a week after the movie, her mother and grandmother both said she had become much more vocal at home and with her friends since the movie. Indeed, three years later in another MOVIExperience, she opted to play the outspoken girl.

The impact can also show up immediately. In Worcester, after a MOVIExperience, the case workers at Centro Las Americas noticed that the girls' hygiene improved. They were dressing better. They were smiling more. And talking more to each other. The staff now sees these foster-home girls standing up for what they think.

Girls with lots of advantages also get a different picture of themselves. One wealthy girl with a chip on her shoulder became fascinated by the way the camera worked. She has now been studying with a female videographer ever since. The chip is where it belongs— in the camera!

How MOVIExperience Works

I showed one movie to a mainstream movie producer. When I casually mentioned that it had been done in four hours with non-actors, he simply didn't believe me. Why does it work? Why can the group come to agreement on so many decisions in such a short time? Why do the girls set aside their egos and sprint to make the movie come out right? Why do they cooperate with girls they've argued with in the past? I have a few ideas. Something magic happens during the Brainstorm, when the girls see their collective ideas melding into a real story. I can feel it. We lift off. At that moment, the story takes over and it's more important than each individual. We are then all in service to the story—the girls, the staff, the coach, the volunteers. We're swept up, and it doesn't set us down until the last scene is shot.

The girls learn the skills and rules for brainstorming. Once the story is figured out, they see how their ideas fit together into a cohesive whole. They can trace, for example, where one of their own ideas led to the theme of the movie or a character or a scene that becomes pivotal. The group often experiences a shift into *group mind* where group members are invested in the group idea and assume ownership of the whole movie, not just their piece of it. Often, far more is possible in this fluid atmosphere than could ever be predicted or scripted.

Our goal is to offer MOVIExperience programs to as many girls as possible. So we continually seek funding to offer programs. Organizations also work hard to bring us in. The Sisters Inc. board of directors saw an article on ACT NOW! and invited us to make a presentation. The women who had started this mentoring program for the hill towns of Western Massachusetts were very impressed with how our philosophy fit in with their mission. Having no money in their budget didn't stop them. They personally raised the money. Their fervor resulted in more than they hoped, and ACT NOW! facilitated a splendid MOVIExperience for 15 girls and their mentors.

ACT NOW! generally works with 30 participants for a total of 13 contact hours. Preparation and other behind-the-scenes work can take up to an additional 40 hours for the ACT NOW! team over several months—depending on the options elected.

Once a group calls us, we design a program that works best for them: goals, budget, and time frame. We start with the basic MOVIExperience. That entails: a facilitated Brainstorm with the players; an instructional tape of games called Coach's Signals, and a customized scenario, based on the story and characters the players invent. It also involves assistance with publicity; a full day of shooting; a screening of the entire movie immediately after the last scene is done, and a one-year membership in The Interacters, a group interested in improv and movie making, which is being formed by ACT NOW! and Group Creativity Projects, Inc.

And finally, it includes the (unedited) movie, which is usually about 20 minutes long. We can add other options such as documentation of the entire process, a facilitated debriefing, a sweetened final tape with music, title and credits, and special screening with certificates. Using all the written materials provided during the process, groups can use the method independently in their programs. More information about ACT NOW! is available at www.actnow-online.org.

16 Lessons— Some Easy, Some Hard

Every Project Manager fantasizes about working with a group that cannot make its own movie but has boundless energy, life experience, feeling—that is, talent. My fantasy goes like this.

Participants screen the tape to see what they look like, what they sound like, whether their thing appears to be a movie. I ask: "Did you enjoy playing that scene?" or "Can you follow the story we told?" If they say, "yes," I've done my job.

Boomerang Kids

First shot on Long Island, this short movie grew out of a remark by Charlie Raebeck, who said he'd support anything artistic— provided it was sincere. I ran an improv workshop for him and Audrey in their living room. Half the players wanted to join the next MOVIExperience—111 miles away in New York City.

After a 4-hour drive, the Long Island group more or less stepped out of their car and onto the camera. They were surprised how fast the story went. Four and a half hours later, the Raebecks would invite some of their 8 kids to see the tape screened.

We were lucky: how many dangers we skirted! The first improv hinted at sexual domination. In the clamorous laundry scene body language took over where audio failed. The Day Care scene refused to bog down in wet diapers. And of the three desperate children coming home with big problems, not one problem rang false. Not once did Michael DiPaolo have to rewind and delete Take I.

All of our locations were 5 minutes or less from Home Base. We skirted melodrama. The gritty scenes were a setup for the question: "How did this happen in such a nice family?"

Best of all, some players were turned on by the experience. They paid attention when I said, "The movie we're shooting is not important. What's important is friendships made today and at shoots in the future."

Half the cast I would see again.

Gristede's Versus Writers

Gristede's Supermarket is mostly men—in their twenties or thirties, some in college. All skilled—keeping a grocery running from 6 a.m. to 11 p.m.

After shopping there for 25 years, I confided to Pete, a new Assistant Manager, that his staff was great: they had the brains to make a short movie. He agreed. Whenever I went shopping, he'd stop working to rap about *our movie*. Staff would walk by—he'd recruit guys for our movie. The Deli Manager was going to be in our movie. The stubby cashier was, too.

In the narrow aisles Pete did gross imitations of TV performers while I came up with questions about reality:

"Will they let us shoot in the store?"

"Why not?"

"Where can we get women players?"

"Leave it to me."

"We have to sit down for an hour in Washington Square, find out what scenes the guys want to play into."

"Sure."

Meanwhile I watched Pete's relationships with staff. Many were precisely on his wavelength, which was speedy. He made constant puns about sports, musical celebrities, TV shows. I couldn't wait to get him on camera.

His relationship with customers: excellent. One evening he had a brilliant conversation with a spacy white customer: a cameo that could go right into any movie. But as for coming up with one idea for a scene: no luck.

As for the guys, ask them if they're going to be in the movie, they say, "Definitely." On the other hand, give them a news flash ("We're shooting in the Square Saturday 2 p.m."), I get a blank stare.

Hooked by now, I decided the movie is coming off—even if I have to involve my workshop.

I took scenario writers in my group to the store and gave them an assignment: "Wander down the aisles, until you hit on a scene that would work for this place."

The response was effusive, for instance:

- The movie is about a couple spending their honeymoon on Aisle 3.
- A customer is sucked through the label into a pineapple can.
- Customers gripped by smells of olives & curry are whisked to faraway islands.

I realize this is abstract fantasy. Can't they come up with one scenario that the guys could play into?

So I myself come up with a scenario on:

Getting Over

An employee gets over on the manager by inventing an artful excuse for being late. Together guys get over on 100-pound sacks they stack in the basement. In the freezer a guy gets over on a girl by getting her phone number....

I ask Pete to play the manager with us in Washington Square.

We did perform, but without the supermarket. At last I realized what Pete & the guys loved was the *idea* of making a movie. They could imagine running a store, but they couldn't imagine inventing a scene, playing themselves or somebody else, creating a story that came from them.

The group that came up with ideas was also lightyears away from a supermarket movie. Their honeymoon idea would close the store down! Players popping into cans would cost $50,000 in special effects! Spice Islands? Forget it!

E.J. Palven Group

We met on the Upper East Side for a sumptuous Saturday lunch cooked by E.J. Half of those who showed up were from my group, half from hers. Many guests didn't come because of sporadic rainfall, but the nine of us felt secure even with no scenario. Why?

We had a lot in common, being New Yorkers in tune with improv (rather than standup). The difference is this:

Improv explores themes & relationships; the material shapes the outcome. Standup nails an experience to the bottom line, which is the laugh. If there's no laugh, the experience is thrown out and replaced; the outcome shapes the material.

As people entered the apartment, I asked them to play a character game: pick a card with opposite characteristics written on it and go with one of the two. You are a bishop, for instance, and an intellectual mechanic. This they did before even taking off their coats.

After lunch we sat around the kitchen and traded ideas, most of which had to do with fraudulent research and lonely people meeting by phone. A lethargic Brainstorm. Almost everyone came up with ideas: none of them got critiqued.

Suddenly E.J. jumped—like a little girl feeling a tug on her fishing line. "I've got it! Oh, I've got it! A professor offers a short intensive course on the Art of Failure."

Everyone went along with this premise, not because E.J. was our hostess, but because her idea was feasible and relevant. It related to our *learning centers* with courses on reflexology and Tibetan chant.

Exterior locations were not crucial. Darra, who was picked for the part of professor, is in educational administration. He chose an Italian character, giving off gusto while justifying his bizarre approach:

"I gave these course already—inna Bologna."

The Italian aura also explained the man's innocence as he approached students with dangerous psychological deficits:

A 60-year-old was dying to divorce her family—never to see them again; a 35-year-old was a paranoid and at the same time famished for male affection; a 30-year-old had made his sex life dependent on political outcomes over which he had no control.

In the next 4 hours we filled out a scenario, picking locations as we moved along. My son Evan shot 10 scenes of some 2 minutes each. The rain came and went. We shot outdoors twice, returned to E.J.'s, and saw our tape.

Why was this session a success? I'd say because of E.J.'s food, which was a powerful magnet, and her wit, which is sharp.

For me this sequence is a model:
- game
- lunch
- training
- Brainstorm (improvised scenario)
- shooting schedule with locations on stone stoop, staircase, living room, street, parlor

My group came out for many more shoots, but the other group was not sold on moviemaking. Once again I see: bridge players often like each other better than bridge, group moviemakers may like each other more than moviemaking.

Once people understand that they can make their own move, will they drop bingo, bridge, golf, and watercolors? No. But they will have a richer and more meaningful array of choices.

500 Nations, Chicago

I was told by Paul Donahue that the place to go in Pilsen, a Mexican-American neighborhood in Chicago, was 500 Nations. When I phoned, a waiter showed interest in my movie project. So when I arrived to meet the owner, Saul Maravilla, things were already in place.

"What do you want the movie to be about?" I asked Saul.

"Gentrification," he said, simply.

I didn't realize what a hot, serpentine, political theme I'd accepted.

My first stop was Father Dahm, who assured me: "There is no gentrification in Pilsen, Mr. Shepherd. But in 5 years *there will be.*"

I heard, again & again, that real estate money was going to sweep every Mexican-American out of Pilsen—except those few who owned their own homes. The villains were described as yuppies, who could afford to pay $1000 per month rent in order to live closer to their offices in the Loop.

Our Production Assistants—Samson, Mable, McDonald—started to lay out the story of gentrification. It ran from Developer to Housing Inspector to Contractors (bidding on repairs) to impoverished Owner, who sells out to Developer.

In a Laundromat we found piles of talent, then realized no one there had a phone! (It's dangerous on a shoot not to be able to reach people—when plans change.)

Martha led me to a barbecue, where I met a dozen people who all had phones, but they couldn't express the day-to-day anxiety of the jobless Spanish-speaking immigrant.

To get my leading man, I had to go with Saul to Casa Aztlan, where we made a presentation to a GED class. We got 4 volunteers and took Carmelo, who looked like he could work in a factory, and Maria, who spoke little English and had two kids. Maria disappeared immediately—afraid of insulting Carmelo's wife if she played his wife.

I changed "wife" to "cousin."

To find Carmelo's "cousin," I looked for actors in a local stage production. That's where I met Miguel, then Susana, who looked, talked and acted the part.

I was now fully cast. But I'd forgotten that in MOVIExperience you take whatever appears.

We shot 3 times more than usual because we felt our tape was important. It would be used at the GED classes, community agencies, schools.

We showed a rough cut at the café. A dozen customers watched. Each opinion conflicted with the next. The most convincing viewer was Anna Marie, who told us we'd missed the point: the point was *struggle*. How to sort out & respond to this feedback?

I believed a half dozen inserts could be shot to be sent East for edit. I asked 3 group members if they could give 4 hours. I sent out a storyboard.

"Now does this story ring true?" I ask.

The answer: Tilda enrolls in college. McDonald disappears into a night job to pay debts. Sampson falls out of love with video. Sutherland buys an old house and has to plaster it. Donahue is finishing a video thesis on the KKK. One key member of the group lands in jail.

My project had turned into a major production.

I'd abandoned MOVIExperience! Instead of playing freely with a group, I was casting cautiously. Instead of training players to make decisions, I was making most decisions myself. Instead of guaranteeing fun, I was diving into serious sociology.

Instead of an organic process to share with people, I had a video cassette to distribute.

17 Interviews with the Experts

Sutherland Talks to Shepherd about Sound

Dan Sutherland is a playwright, teacher, and independent video producer.

After eager moviemakers purchase their decks, they are not going to want to run out and spend more money. But where in their budget is sound? They think their very ambitious projects can be covered by the little internal camera mic, called the on-board mic. This apparatus is limited in frequency, low in power, and housed right next to powerful machines driving the tape forward. Machines make noise.

How can the on-board mic record the voice 15 feet away of a teenage woman, tapping a neighing horse with a riding crop as bees buzz off honeysuckle and somewhere a baseball game is playing on TV?

Your internal mic records much of this, but the different sounds melt together and the volume is bound to be low: you will crane your head at the screen until you get tired and turn the tape off.

Your internal mic will, of course, pick up music, but it will probably sound tinny when played back on a TV speaker or projector. Your mic will pick up dialog, but the volume will probably be so low that you can't boost it in duping or post-production. As for the sound of waves, volleyball players and gulls at the beach, you might not be able to distinguish one from another if recorded with an on-board mic.

What the little mic is giving you is little. What you need is a lot—of excellence. Not possible with the on-board mic. The way to go is to get off your butt, call a few places, drive from specialty store to specialty store and choose the microphone that will make you happy—an external mic, held on a boom as close as possible to the source of sound without its appearing in the video frame.

An external mic will require the services of one person during a shoot. But you can justify that by saying you need an extra hand who can also help out in many other ways. If you can't round up this Assistant Sound Person, then buy a superior mic that sits on your camera, not inside.

Editing on a computer and duping at home

If you aren't editing now, you probably will be by Christmas. See our Bibliography for editing manuals.

When you edit you'll become much more aware of

- the number of sound sources, plus
- sound sources that could be deleted, plus
- sound sources that could be added.

You'll start thinking how you would ideally design the sound that envelopes the action, and how the action could be changed to accommodate your design. You'll get creative.

Good sound should have a sense of fidelity. If a room sounded crisp and hard (a dance room or a tiled bathroom) that is the way it should sound. It should sound that way. If a room sounded soft from carpeting and drapes, the sound should represent this reality.

Choosing a Mic

How much will you spend? Where will you go window-shopping? Where you shop shows what kind of videographer you are.

- If you order online, we know you don't want to have a discussion.
- If you go to Radio Shack, we know you like limited choices.
- If you go to a specialty store, we know you're looking to find the real deal, even though you may not buy anything there.

Types of Mics

There are only two types you have to choose from. Dynamic relies on aural dynamism. Condenser relies on a charge from a battery in the mic or the recording device.

There are two types of mic patterns: omnidirectional and directional. The latter is sometimes called a cardiod or a shotgun.

Condenser and dynamic mics can be either cardiod or omni. But a shotgun is usually battery powered, and the omni is usually dynamic.

Which one is best for you? Okay, here's a rule of thumb. Dynamic mics can take more abuse. Condensers capture high tones, but they eat batteries, and the batteries have to be turned off even if you're taking a short break in the shoot.

How do you determine if a battery is up to charge? There's a battery tester you can buy, of course, or you can slip it into a flashlight to see if it produces a bright light.

How can you tell if your mic is working? Some videomakers assume their internal mic is always working; they never review footage. Get in the habit of working with a headset on, or putting a headset on at a break in the shoot. What you're looking for is signal-to-noise ratio.

Signal to Noise. The Signal should be clear, discernable, and free from interference. What sounded intelligible during production should sound the same during playback.

With any Signal comes Noise. Noise will always be on the recording in some form. It comes from the media (for example, tape or CD) and from the hardware itself (transistors, line cords, wire wrapped around the magnet, adapters).

Adapters, like mics, are to be bought at a high-end audio or specialty retailer. It's a question of machine tolerance. How well were the parts machined? I buy adapters from the manufacturer of the camera or the manufacturer of the mic.

Multiple adapters? Use as few as possible. The more you adapt, the more likely you'll have a short or a broken signal.

Placing the Mic

Some cameras have on-board attachments for a mic. They limit the area you're trying to cover. They can also be subject to vibrational noise from the camera. My best sound comes from a boom operator who has the mic on a fish pole. Attachments? You could create a shock mount that absorbs vibration.

The best sound comes from pointing at the throat of the person speaking, which is lower than most manufacturers recommend.

Who should you pick to focus on? Is it the loudest player? Is it the person with the most lines? Is it the person who is dead center? As primary sonic target, I'd choose the person with the weakest voice. If you do you'll always have that person's signal, and the others will be on target by virtue of their sonic authority.

There are factors that influence sound. Humidity will take the edge off a recording. So will people in crowds. How do you discover this? Sound dropout, buzzing and impedance noise (from electrical devices) are not evident on your $5 headset. So play back with a headset that has a quality like what you want your video to have.

Your playback, for instance, will catch distortion. That's a condition coming from too much signal trying to fit onto too little media. Distortion sound, which is mildly acceptable with analog (VHS), digital can't handle. It turns the distorted signal to mud. Once you've recorded any distorted signal, it is there. And it can't be fixed.

Music

There are two types of music on the planet: copyrighted and not copyrighted. The former is owned and has to be negotiated for. The latter may be public domain—like a lot of folk music written during the last century. In which case, it is yours. Some uncopyrighted music falls into the grey area of a negotiable commodity. There are young lawyers whose job is to find movies that use copyrighted material that has not been contractually cleared. There are also Web sites where you can find more music than you can possibly use for the rest of your life. There are CDs made to be gobbled up in productions just like yours.

A Final Word

The last job you have to do is to listen to your video piece on a good pair of speakers. Just because the output looks good on the monitor, doesn't mean it will sound good when you hear it on a decent system.

Coken Talks with Sutherland about Sound

Rick Coken is on the Columbia College faculty in Chicago.

Dan Sutherland: How do you make your sound package cost effective?

Rick Coken: Shoot single system. That is, record both picture and sound on the same medium. Don't cheap out on the microphone. If you record separately on an audiotape recorder, you're forced to go into postproduction, which takes a lot of time and eats up money. Avoid it.

D: About postproduction, they say if you record a digital audio track, it always stays in sync with the video track.

R: That's a lie. It will drift and it will wander, and you'll look like you're making Godzilla again. Sync problems.

D: Where can we get reliable advice? Say we're buying a mid-range deck.

R: Go to a professional shop, not a chain store. Professional shops do sell low-end gear, their advice is professional, and it costs you nothing.

D: What do you do with actors who are mismatched on their decibel output?

R: Where you place the mic will help balance the volume level between the talent. If you ask the talent to balance, you're going to kill their delivery. Because you're now directing them into a technology delivery instead of an art form. Don't do that. Try to work it out with the microphone. The other thing obviously is multiple microphones, plus a mic mixer. But now you've taken costs up to almost professional levels.

D: Do you recommend a GC (automatic gain control)?

R: The biggest pitfall of the low-budget moviemaker: they try to do everything in whatever mode of automatic. The signal can never be fixed. For instance, you have one shot to capture this moment, and if automatic is not working properly, you cannot recover. Automatic is purely amateur; it's for recording the kids' birthday where people really don't care what it sounds like. Avoid that at all costs.

D: What about sound on location?

R: Sometimes a moviemaker goes out and finds the best location possible for the shoot: sweet, great light, great background, nice furniture.

Close your eyes: use your ears, and listen: wonderful, at 5 p.m., just birds and this quiet neighborhood. Well, we shoot at 1 p.m. Four blocks away, this construction site starts up! Bulldozers, cranes, pile drivers. So always scout the location at the same time of day you're going to shoot.

Don't plan a love scene, "Honey I love you," under the L tracks during rush hour. You're doomed. Start using all your senses when you're scouting locations—especially your ears. And note the time of day because it's going to make a difference in the location's ambient sound.

D: How does the moviemaker get low-budget advice?

R: When you go shopping, don't start the conversation by saying, "I'm trying to go low budget." No, you're trying to be "cost effective." You want to put out this unique video, so you want some semblance of quality. Put the salespeople in the right domain; otherwise they pull out everything high-end. When they see you coming, they often know when you're not a high-end user. That's OK. There's no reason for embarrassment. There are more low-end users than high-end users. So long as they have the stuff on the shelf, terrific. And they're always willing to talk.

Experts Talk about Lighting

Mark Siska and Ilko Davidov talk with David Shepherd about lighting.

David Shepherd: How much should a video movie group spend on lighting?

Ilko Davidov: My budget would depend on what scenes we do in what locations according to what script; how many players are in a scene and what the action is. Then rent equipment.

D: So rig the lights in order to illuminate the people on camera today.

ID: Sure.

Mark Siska: To go professional you'll spend about $1000 for a decent light kit. You can also utilize existing light—indoors or outdoors. Video is so sensitive that often you can use whatever light is there. Just white balance your camera and then set your exposures correctly so you don't get blown out (too light) or look brown. Use some kind of fill light for the face, or a clamp-on floodlight so your background doesn't get muddy. You're looking at maybe two lights. Or, if you're working a small room, just bounce the light around and keep it consistent.

D: Bounce it off the ceiling?

MS: Yes. If it's 750 watts, it's going to be bright. That's like a film light. But first decide: what is your aesthetic, your style?

D: Do we try to give an actress indoors the same luminosity she has in the sun?

ID: If the scene takes place in the evening, use way less light, but don't compromise the quality of her image.

D: Are you too against grain, Mark?

MS: I deal with it in postproduction. I go for the best lighting condition and then adjust it in edit. That's another thing you can do if you have uneven light, which you will have if you don't know how to light a scene. In postproduction you can always do a basic color correction where you kind of correct the light, itself. But don't be too concerned with postproduction. First get the fundamentals of lighting or at least a style so you don't have to always fix everything in postproduction.

ID: You cannot fix it in postproduction if the scene is too grainy—unless you want it grainy on purpose.

D: The books say you should always have a key light, a filler light, and then a third smaller light. Do you go for that formula?

MS: If you have natural lighting, shooting by daylight, you can usually get away with that. You can also use natural light as fill to a key light. What kind of imagery do you like? Do you like the way the frame looks with big contrast, stark, or even? There are so many looks. Which one do you want to capture on video?

D: The camera is smart, but it's not going to talk to you, "Hey, there's not enough light on that woman's face." How do we know there's not enough?

MS: The camera also allows you to measure your light. Have a look and see if the woman is too dark or blown out. Then compensate by adjustment.

ID: If you're on a tight budget and you don't want to use a lot of lights, choose your locations very carefully and look at them through the camera before you actually do the shoot.

D: Choose your locations carefully means...?

ID: Make sure locations have enough natural light—for example, from the window if you're shooting indoors. If you can't afford to buy expensive fixtures, use the lamps in your home with 200W or 300W bulbs.

D: How do you handle silhouettes?

MS: Don't stick your figure directly in backlight because it will not look natural. Be careful following action if your figure walks in front of the light and then out of the light. Some cameras won't accept the extreme change in lighting.

D: What if you don't want to risk silhouettes?

ID: Light from the front or the side to equalize the brightness of the backlight.

MS: When you shoot right in front on a face, it's going to look flatter than if you move the light to the side—creating contrast and a shadow

ID: Do a lot of tests. Know what your latitude is. Sometimes if you have greater latitude, from dark to bright, it's easier to avoid having silhouettes. So, know the light sensitivity of the optics of your camera. Every brand is different.

What do you do when you have only a few lights and you're shooting a large space like a warehouse? How do you make sure players don't disappear into darkness?

ID: I put masking tape on the floor and tell them they cannot go a certain way, unless they have a reason to be in the shadows.

D: Suppose you have a car with a driver and a passenger. The car is rolling from darkness into brilliant light. How do you light that?

MS: It all depends on what look you want to get. Do you want more pronounced shadows? Where do you want the light source— from inside the car or outside? It depends on how dark you want to make it look. Do tests. Play around.

ID: Most professionals will light a car while it's static. But for low-budget movies it's probably best to have the car moving in a well lit section of the street. Or create shadows artificially to create motion.

D: How do you light a discotheque?

MS: If you walk into red light, remember: it doesn't respond well to video. Find that area of the disco with the most light—the bar and some portion of the dance floor. Go with that and hopefully by looking at it, you'll find how to shut your shutter correctly. It's hard.

ID: Make sure the faces can be seen. You don't want a bunch of figures where you can't tell who is who. If it's just dancing, then it depends on bodies alone. But if there's conversation, I'd make sure there's a bunch of candles on the table.

D: How do you shoot candles?

ID: Bring the camera in close; it's pretty sensitive. Getting the candles to throw out enough light to light up a face might be an issue.

D: Suppose you have a séance with a ring of people, and you want to light only one of the faces.

MS: Make the scene subdued with maybe a light bouncing off the ceiling. Play with light and shadow to get enough light on the one face. If you have to, pull in barn doors or a scrim or some kind of diffused light. Try gels if you want a more yellow mood.

D: Can lighting create emotion?

MS: It depends on the scene. If you're doing Sci-Fi you might slip a green gel in front of your lighting instrument. Gels are good at throwing out a backlight or adding color to a scene. Say you're in natural light with a white wall that doesn't say anything, a gel might make your boring shot exciting because you're adding another dimension through light. You're creating a backdrop through light.

D: Do you have experience evoking emotion through light?

ID: Within the same scene I've lit people many ways as their emotion changed. I used close-ups.

D: How would you light a cloudy day?

ID: Recreate the natural environment of the place. I would use a top light overhead.

MS: Anyone interested in lighting should look at Flemish art. It deals with situations, people, their interactions with light. In a Flemish painting you see a light source coming in through a window, then breaking up. Try to recreate that though video. You get a perspective of how light interacts with environment in a natural way.

D: How would you light an underground escape tunnel leading away from a prison? Would you use that little spotlight fixed to the top of the camera, for example?

ID: I would not; they create hot spots in the dark, where nothing is lit except what's right in front of you. When you move the camera, the light moves with the camera, and this makes the scene unbelievable for the viewer. Lights should be steady. I would backlight the action in this tunnel. Light should come from behind the players, putting them in silhouette. Maybe I'll throw behind me a lowlight playing over faces and eyes. This would be a small light, and I'd want players to move in and out of it.

D: Enough, guys. You've given me a lot to look at and think about the next time I see one of your movies. Thank you.

David Shepherd created Chicago COMPASS and today runs Group Creativity Projects out of Belchertown, MA.

Mark Siska runs the international film exhibition, Eurounderground, out of Chicago. In 2003 its focus is Berlin.

Ilko Davidov is co-owner of a film services group in Chicago—Bullet Proof Film.

George Kuchar

George Kuchar talks with David Shepherd about his strategies for making improvisational films.

David: George, what's the role of improv in your work? By improv, I mean extempore. Everything: dialog, scenario, casting, locations...

George: Every time I go out I improvise. I have the ideas, not a script, so I write dialog for the students while they're getting madeup. Or I ask them to write dialog for a scene we shoot that day.

D: How do you warm up the players?

G: They warm up by getting into their costumes, while I say, "Hurry up. We have no time. We have to get this done."

D: What's the average age?

G: From high school up. Also I have some in their twenties who bring parents. We put the parents into a role.

D: I've been told the more detailed the characters, the better the movie. True?

G: Sometimes you choose their clothes, hair, makeup. You design the picture for them. Create a Marlene Dietrich, you know?

D: I'm told drama is the refuge of fantasy while documentary is the nose of reality.

G: It's all fake. You always have the impulse to make it look better. Or worse. Depends on your state of mind.

D: OK...here's your shrimp toast coming, George...How many narrative pieces have you made?

G: Two a year since '80.

D: How many of those were edited in camera?

G: Three quarters.

D: How long does it take you to make a narrative?

G: We meet once a week for 6 hours over a semester 3 months long.

D: The class is how big?

G: From 8 to 32.

D: How big is your staff?

G: One assistant. Along about the third week, when students get an idea of what the picture will look like, I have second- and third-unit crews go out. Whenever I don't want to be in a room with so many people, I hand out assignments.

D: Suppose you want to send me out. What do you say to me?

G: First of all, you have to come to me, and say, "What do you want me to do?" And I say, "Well look, we need a Second Unit scene—a love scene in a space station. Why don't you get a camera and somebody to work it? Invite this actor and our guest." (See that's 4 people gone.) Plus a Location Manager—5 people gone.

D: Do you have a Continuity Person?

G: There's no continuity—just a general idea. Most of our people don't know what's going on most of the time.

D: So you shoot and insert corrective segments. How long does a Kuchar movie run?

G: Between 20 and 45 minutes. Like all of a sudden someone will say, "I want to be a vampire." The picture gets longer because we write in a vampire scene and try to explain why it's there. In another class some guy says, "Let's have a wrestling sequence" because he's into wrestling. OK. Pretty soon we have 20 cassettes of wrestling. How to tie it all together? I let them find the answer: the cast is in a movie production company that's doing both horror and a wrestling series. Like the Aztec Mummy—wrestling.

D: You accommodate any desire they have by changing the plot.

G: This also helps them feel they're getting it off their chest, becoming complete somehow. They have this obsessive fantasy, which we bring on screen.

D: Who's in your national audience?

G: Anyone interested in comics and low-budget picture making.

D: You get distributed?

G: Through Video Data Bank in Chicago (info@vdb.org)

D: What does it cost to make one of these things?

G: I have an $800 budget from the college.

D: I made "Shanty Queen" at $100 per minute; 35 minutes. Ambitious.

G: San Francisco College of the Arts discourages anything commercial. Students take a camera out. Then they have to learn how to use it. Next they take out lights, so now they have to learn how to make a scene look dramatic. If we have an earthquake sequence, they learn to work in miniature. It's all about fixing problems. At a certain point they have to act. They can't always do it. But we try to make them appear the best possible or, the worst, whichever looks better.

D: Let's take a break. (Here, let me add that in "Reflections from a Cinematic Cesspool" Kuchar asserts that scenarios are pointless:

the only reason to make a movie is to discover something—whatever it is the group has inside itself.)

D: How do you control the class?

G: Act as if you're in control. It's a performance. Sometimes they ask how to work the camera, and I just don't know. I go blank. I send students out to shoot a background that's real, bring it back and project it. It's totally fake! But that gives me a little more control.

D: I get the impression you are always in control thanks to your imagination, which gives you the power to change anything.

G: My ultimate control is editing. Then I can make the picture look as good as it can be.

D: During the class you seem to control the story.

G: It has to be that way because a lead actor may not show up. Sometimes they get sick of coming. I don't threaten anyone with failure because, look, it should be a swinging-door policy. If you're not there willingly, then your bad vibes rub off onto others. So when they show up, we grab them, shoot their whole scene in two hours.

D: You get over—always.

G: The main thing is always to have footage. If you do, you can concoct something after the fact. At the screening students might say, "What the hell is this?" They didn't know it was going to turn out this way. Neither did I.

D: Do you ever clash with a student?

G: Sure. I say, "That's a good idea. Here's another." Then we pick one.

D: Do you teach them how to make movies on their own?

G: Yes, because I do tutorial, where I sit down with students, see how they can fix their picture, realize it.

D: About the movie you sent me, "Vile Cargo." It seems to be "camp" attitudes of the 30's.

G: You know what happens. We do have a story, but the people thrown into it can't act. We find we're laughing. It seems funny, but we never try to shoot it so it will come out intentionally funny.

D: I had the same experience in Hadley, Mass. Students wanted to do "self-destruction." It came out quite amusing.

G: The cast for "Vile Bodies" was so big that characters from previous scenes were brought back—just to cover up sections of the tape that were no good. We were layering.

D: Want to talk about the way you direct? Like, by giving suggestion, blocking, pacing, digging the family dynamic...

G: The whole idea is to make it look like big drama. People behave a certain way when they're in big drama, like spinning around fast to face the other player.

Some people look good when they don't act at all. Sometimes we have them just move the lips, while another actor off camera talks into a mic.

D: That scene where the daughter is in bed dying of starvation, and the mother is making excuses about not being able to please a man, how did you direct that?

G: That was Karen Redgreen—completely undirectable. She has to follow the script to the letter even though I'm the one who wrote it.

D: (LAUGHS)

G: My directing would be to frame them in the fake set and make it all look balanced.

D: You cut from that bedside scene to the mother making a tape recording?

G: I had people interrupt to make comments on scenes that they'd been in. I developed that style for editing in camera (scene/comment, scene/comment). The picture was well liked in Iowa by German intellectuals, while local students were appalled by the subject matter.

D: Which scenes that you direct give you the most pleasure?

G: A man picking things up, sitting, putting his foot onto a desk, walking over to the wall, turning around... Makes you think, "Boy, that guy sure is being directed."

D: Suppose an actor simply doesn't get it?

G: If they're completely off, they stand out. Let them do their own rendition. Then everybody gets a big kick out of it.

D: What do professionals do that amateurs can't do, and what do amateurs do that professionals can't?

G: Professionals yell at each other: "How come you're not here on time?" "You're not paying attention." "You're just standing around." An Amateur says, "Thank you for being in my picture."

D: Why are you doing movies?

G: I've always wanted to make them, so I'll make them any way I can. There are lots of people who want to be in movies, and they'll be in them any way they can. If we're all stuck in the same place, like at school, with some kind of formula that people want to use on a project, just do it. It's an excuse to live that dream.

D: I'm ready to work in a dozen areas, from golf clubs to prisons.

G: I see it nowadays in back yards—kids out there with equipment, making their own pictures. Making friends.

D: Apple Computer is promoting home editing by FireWire. Do you have anything to say about editing in camera?

G: I like it. It's like live TV. It has a panic quality: the camera is programmed to go off on an insert shot. You know you have 50 seconds to do a take, so you rehearse real quick, then shoot it. There's certain edge and intensity to it.

D: JVC puts out a camcorder that makes clean video inserts. I love editing in camera; I think it's like Japanese art—minimalist. I ran a contest, but contestants didn't take it seriously. One guy stuck the camera over his head and ran through a gay section of Chicago. How about editing in studio?

G: I edit in my living room. I bought a nonlinear digital editor. [It] becomes obsessive. You go on hour after hour. You forget when to stop.

D: With a 20-minute narrative: how long would that take you?

G: Depends on how much you doctor up the picture. It can go from 3 days...

D: 36 hours?

G: Start maybe at 3 p.m. and stop 1 a.m.—taking one break. Next day start 5 p.m. and end at midnight.

D: The stuff you showed 200 of us at the Walter Reed theatre was exquisitely appropriate. Its different styles dovetailed nicely. Then you spoke about how to put the stuff together—teaching us at the same time you were showing us models of your work. Suppose the Rockefellers gave you $100,000.

G: I'd buy some nice equipment. Make a picture with nice dresses. Experiment.

D: Suppose you wanted to double your money, and you had the right script.

G: My pictures drag the producer into the mud—know what I mean? If you made back the money, it would all go into the next picture.

D: What experience would you like to have in the next 20 years?

G: Milk whatever I got going now before the curtain comes down.

D: "Curtain comes down!" You are youthful, vital; your twin brother is alive. Your mother is alive.

G: I'd like to use my equipment before it gets stolen or the house burns down. That damn editor is sitting there, and it's fun to use. It's saying, "Let's make another picture."

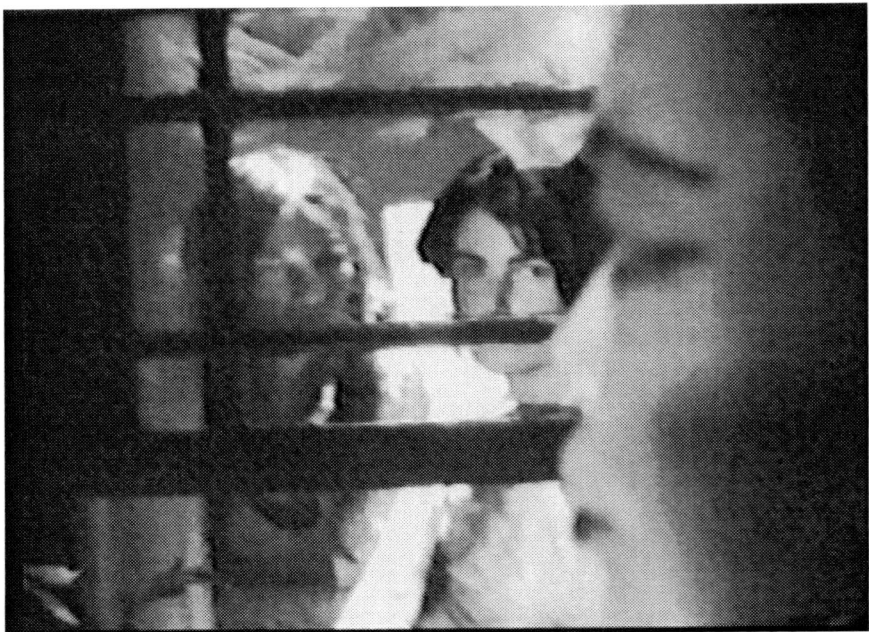

Figure 36. "Vile Cargo" by George Kuchar, 1990. Note the meticulous detail arrived at through catch-as-catch-can technology. George stays close to improv.

George Kuchar grew up in the Bronx, making 8mm movies. He earned enough money to switch to 16mm in 1965. In 1970 he was invited to teach filmmaking at the San Francisco Art Institute, becoming a traitor to his department when 8mm video won him away from celluloid. Once a year he goes to the Midwest, waits patiently in a motel until tornadoes form and do their thing in front of his camera. Some of his movies are entitled "Hold Me while I'm Naked," "Color me Shameless," "Lust for Ecstasy." His video pieces include diaries & portraits of places with live inhabitants: "Vile Cargo," "Fill thy Crack with Whiteness."

John Fucile

David Shepherd talks to John Fucile about directing improvisational features on video.

David: OK, we're here with John Fucile. I want to ask rudimentary questions, like how do you cast? How do you decide among twelve people that you're going to use these six and not those six?

John: Well, for any sort of video piece, I look for iconic types, so to speak. I use not necessarily actors, but people who I think represent a particular role. I tend to cast on an outline of someone, on how he or she strikes you physically.

D: Well, suppose you're working with people you never saw before. How would you figure which ones can fulfill your vision?

J: Now that's an interesting question. Probably, I would explore, through a series of questions, who they'd be willing to play and what they'd be willing to do. I'd start off having them tell me about themselves. If you're going to use someone for a part, you need to know who they are. So, I'd have them just sort of open up. I don't believe in auditioning off a text.

D: Tell me about that.

J: You're asking someone to participate in a collective; that's what I think video making is. It's not an entrepreneurial deal where you just get to run, like a dictator, over everyone. I think players are part of the process. You have to find out who the person is so you can either break down their walls or exploit them in comfort.

D: Say you have five minutes to give a screen test. What do you do?

J: Ask them to tell me about themselves, why they're here, what they want to get out of it. I like desperation. That's my thing. I like someone who desperately communicates whatever it is they need to express through jazz, dance, acting, voice, whatever. I need to see some absolute commitment. Not to think they want to do it, but they have no other choice. You can see it immediately...it's not "please hire me!" It's the massive desire. That would be my first clue: this someone has something to say. It's surprising how many are trying to get involved for what I consider the wrong reasons. Someone wants to be famous. Someone wants to see themselves on TV. Someone wants just to be part of something. That's different from someone committed to communicating through their own personal medium.

D: How do you cast a specific character?

J: Flipping roles is a great way. Suppose you're asked to play a woman, it's not that you're going to play a genuine woman, but the woman playing opposite you may learn something about her own gender through your character. I think flipping is a very valuable thing: have both players play something they would never do otherwise.

D: Flipping for casting or flipping for performance?

J: Casting. I wouldn't use it in performance. I wouldn't have a four-year old boy play a priest or an old gentleman play a four-year old boy. I think it's a very valuable exercise to flip roles in a "backstory" sort of setting.

D: How do you choose a location and then fix it up and make it work?

John: It's going to sound strange, but I tend to cast my location in a similar way. The location to me speaks as much to the narrative as the actors do. I'm an actor's director, so my cast needs to be in a comfortable place where they can work comfortably, and it needs to be defined as such. I say to the actors, "You can go that far to the light." But, I don't ever work with "Hit your mark. Say your line."

D: Before the players get there, how do you establish this space?

J: For me it's technical. Am I free to be unrestricted in this place? So, I need to be very lateral. I need to have a lot of room, and it's not physical room but emotional room.

D: Say you want to do a scene in a diner. Can you describe what you are looking for? For instance, does it have to do with style, class, or color perhaps?

J: Tough question. I'd say the location is itself a character. It can't be false. It has to be real. It can't be a setup.

D: Do you prefer outdoor or indoor scenes?

J: I like outdoor. Technically, it's a lot more difficult, because you can't control weather, but for some reason, I always find myself outside. I did a music video where we shot on a battleship in Lake Ontario, and we had six inches of freezing rain on the ship. We covered the ship in ice and for eight hours not one crew member asked to leave, because we had all allowed ourselves to be in that location. Once we got there, everyone was totally committed to what was going on. If you commit both the technical crew and the actors to the location, they're with you.

D: Do you use extreme close-ups and extreme long shots?

J: In video? Yeah. I tend to work a circuit when I'm shooting; I think of when the footage will be projected. Coming from a film background, I always think of a face forty feet high on a screen and how that will be viewed. I don't think in video and TV terms, so I watch that my close-ups don't get too tight, because they can look unnatural at points. I like to keep close-ups real natural, not much tighter than forehead-to-chin. But I use a lot of them.

In video, I use long shots as sort of a rehearsal. Let the players flow and act and interact and go back and forth and define the location for themselves within their own personal space. When I use an extreme close-up, I like to see the quality of it before the shoot goes on. I think of an extreme close-up as association to quality. And a long shot I see as environmental and in-relation to. Here's me in a space. Here's my long shot. Here's an extreme close-up; it talks about quality.

D: The quality of the culture? The skin? The coffee cup? Or the quality of the mood?

J: Quality of the object. I relate quality to closeness and a medium shot to the person first in relation to the quality and then in relation to space. For me, video and improv are to set up scenarios in which the choices that are made are inherently correct. Because, you're dealing with the reality in humans. You can't make a wrong choice if you're genuine and you're there.

D: Discovery.

J: You can't hide it. An audience reacts to it, good, bad, or otherwise. They can't help but react.

John Fucile produced "Beat the Blue" and "Zero." He was awarded the Global Vision Award at the 2002 World Population Film and Video Festival, Official Selection at the Ashland Independent Film Festival. He participated in the Big Bear Lake International Film Festival and the Independents Film Festival.

Nancy Fletcher

Donna: Which MOVIExperience was most important to you?

Nancy: The first one, because it opened me up in such a way that I said, 'I want to do this full-time.' I was just so impacted by it, and it was actually my fifty-something birthday, and I had thirty-five friends of mine over testing the format out in the Valley.

D: Describe some of the players.

N: They were part of a group of friends that belonged to a non-geographical-based community, and they were all middle-aged with some teenage children.

D: Could you describe one or two of them, please?

N: Diane Mandle is part French and part Jewish; she speaks fluent French, is extremely talented, has acting background. Annette

Quinones is Puerto Rican and American Indian; beautiful! The theme was a retreat for executives and spouses. But by the time we got to Annette and Diane, they were the last to be cast, so they played a couple. And, they did a very convincing break-up scene in the bathroom.

D: Did this motivate you to do it again?

N: Oh yeah, I wanted to do it all the time. I mean, this has had probably a bigger impact on my life than anything else, because it pointed me to a career that's the culmination of all the careers and experiences I've had to date. And now I'm bringing this to young girls to foster self-esteem.

D: What do you mean you were impacted?

N: It was like a light was lit under me when we did the first MOVIExperience in my house.

D: What were some of the other things that happened?

N: The culmination of the movie: For my birthday people brought flowers, so we handed out daffodils and everybody was waving daffodils. We got in the pool, started singing, and going around in a circle, getting the water to go around in a circle, too. And, it was a real celebration of the theme of the video which was operating outside the box.

D: The corporate box.

N: Yeah. So it was transformational for the players, just as the theme was depicted as a transformational retreat for executives.

D: What did you do the day before?

N: When David walked in he saw my house looked like a retreat, and he came up with the theme of corporate retreat and we discussed that and some other options.

By the time people had to leave, we still hadn't gotten a scenario down. So David said 'Let's get the 3 x 5 cards out and write up some ideas.' So, we did. All night. And when I went to bed, about one, David was still in his room working and when I got up, he was still working on those 3 x 5 cards, thinking about possible scenes.

I had come up with my own bunch of little scenes, and it was fun. But by the time we had our first meeting in the morning with the players, we really didn't have any order for these scenes. So, we gave them to Diane to put in some kind of order.

We had way more scenes than we needed. David took people off immediately and did a car scene. I was in the second scene: guests entered into the 'conference center' where I was one of the greeters. I thought I was supposed to be, like, a 'character,' and I was chewing gum, not being myself.

Karl, who had been recruited to shoot the movie, hadn't arrived. He was coming from New Jersey through snow and sleet, and actually, we had given up on him. But, as the conferees came into the front door with David shooting them, Karl arrived. We were in the middle of shooting, so there was nothing I could do but close the door in his face. The look on his face was absolutely hilarious. Stunned. He had been driving for hours. I slammed the door in his face.

Then, it got dark. There were a couple of cops walking up the driveway. We greeted them because we were in such great spirits. And they said, 'Um, what's going on here?'

We said, 'We're doing a movie. 'Ya wanna be in it?' They were cool cops, and we just kind of swept them right in. We said, 'Can we borrow that flashlight?' And the guy almost gave it to us...He was there because my next-door neighbor had called. Apparently some of our guests had parked in his driveway.

D: There were how many people at the high point?

N: Probably 50, because we had 35 for the shoot and then at least 15 more who came for the screening.

This one guy, Mark Robinson, wanted to get involved in some new way, even after the shoot. So, I said, 'Ya wanna go out and interview all the guests?' He said, 'Yes, sure.' And, I gave him a microphone, which wasn't plugged in to anything. We just pretended it was plugged in. By using it in a very assertive way, he got people's attention time and time again while I put them on camera. That footage is possibly even better than the story footage.

There was a young woman, about 35 years old, who took off her shoes. And, because there was a light snowfall, when she walked on the deck you could see her footprints as she approached a 15-year-old teenager with a beard and put her arms around him and started to kiss him up. He couldn't take it, he bolted. The scene was so appropriate and so unplanned. Nobody told her to do that.

I did a lot of logistics and scene setups, facilitating essentially, and I was having a ball doing it. But, the really wonderful thing about the MOVIExperience, which I don't get now, because I'm at each scene as the Coach, is that you don't know what happened in many scenes until the screening when you get to see how it all fits; it's thrilling. It's like...this wonderful dessert... this wonderful reward at the end, seeing the movie.

There's something about MOVIExperience where you feel reflected in the whole thing. Your ego takes a back seat, and that's why I didn't get upset when my scream got cut in the closet scene.

I remember vividly the next day. This seemed to be almost as important as the first day because we wrapped the tape up. We found credits by shooting different people in an alcove where the CD was located. It had a very natural quality about it.

Annette went in this area and so did Woody, I think, and myself. Karl shot different people messing around with gypsy music. Music makes a huge difference in the final value of a tape.

D: Yeah.

N: I was disappointed in the edited tape. I liked the raw tape best because it showed how the piece fit together with editing in camera. Whoever edited in the Hamptons did some cutesy stuff with it.

D: What feedback did you get from people?

N: They loved it.

D: Then, when did you decide you wanted to do it on your own?

N: I decided almost immediately and had a meeting with Izzy Gesell. We thought we would bring this to corporations as a team-building exercise. Izzy works with corporations anyway, using improv. It turns out he didn't want to do that, because it was too labor intensive, too time consuming, and too low priced. He gets $5000 a shot when he goes out, and all he has to take is his notes and himself...we didn't know how much we could charge for this. Today, I think corporations would pay 10 or 15 thousand dollars, because nonprofits are getting funding to pay 5 thousand.

Charlie Jacobs, who was at the Chicago COMPASS, was counseling me, and he said, "Instead of working with corporations and team building, for which there are plenty of programs, go where there isn't much competition." He said, "Pick the low-hanging fruit, and that's working with girls. Nobody else is doing this with girls and you, would stand out," which is true.

That was in 1998, and I said to Izzy, "It's going to take five years to get this off the ground."

I started by contacting powerful women I know around the country and the world, asking them to be my electronic advisors. All they had to do was receive an e-mail from me every three months about my progress. And, if there was anything about the e-mail they wanted to comment on, they could just click on reply and feed back to me.

So, I created this awareness of our process; this web of people was the very beginning of it. No one knew about this, so I had a lot of spreading the word to do. This was a great way to feel full support, even though my e-visors didn't feel I was leaning on them. It gives me credibility, having this group of women. Then, we formed a board.

D: What do you hope the board will do? What's the most important decision about strategy on the table now?

N: Build a coalition of entities that could support the MOVIExperience and get something back in exchange. That's why I'm going to New York to get a magazine for girls to lend its name (or some advertising space or publicity) plus the manufacturer of a product, like makeup, plus a manufacturer of equipment, and possibly a store that's part of a chain.

I see this could create a nice base of support for, say, a three-year promotion, enabling communities who don't have a lot of money to get subsidized, or get scholarships for their people; get more publicity and more awareness around the county.

D: Ambitious!

N: Somebody suggested Beneton, and I think that's wonderful, because: why stop at the United States? Why not think global?

D: How has MOVIExperience changed you?

N: When I first met David, I was a very tight and controlling person who planned out every single thing ahead of time, pretty much. I never really did anything off the cuff. I was a very scared person who felt there was only one way to do something and I had to find out that one way and then stick to it.

When I first met David, we started brainstorming, and he'd tell me what we needed for the shoot the next day. And this new information was winging in from left field...and I just went with it. I didn't worry. I didn't get crazy that we were out of control. So I just said, "OK, I'll do that."

I was strapped into the moment. And, there was something about MOVIExperience, I guess, or my birthday or something. I started to experience the fact that there's more than one way to do something. It affected every single minute of my life after that. If I was working and I said, "I need to put this up with a paper clip." Still, I didn't get married to that idea. I said, "OK, if I see something, like a bobby pin, I'll use that." I improvised all the time. I just became much more flexible and resourceful. And, that opened up the world to me.

D: Do you remember an event where that happened?

N: On this last shoot, somebody was supposed to fall asleep in mid-bubble bath. We had the bubble bath, and we had the bathing suit, and we had the girl who was willing to go into the bubble bath.

The story, the twenty-scene scenario, is all predicated on this one pivotal scene. Well, it turns out that at the facility we were using, the bathtub didn't work. There was no water. There was no water hooked up. So, we had to change, right then and there. Within two seconds, we had to make a different plan. And, we did: We showed the girl looking in the mirror. And, then we faded to white. We had the apparition appear. Instead of appearing in a dream, we had her appear in the girl's imagination.

D: Right.

N: The apparition said her thing, we faded to white again, and then she disappeared. [Laughs] And, it worked out perfectly!

D: Well, do you think it's David Shepherd's personality that encourages transformation, or the format itself?

N: Both, because David Shepherd is flexible. He's always doing things spontaneously. He makes requests, big requests of people. He goads people to do stuff, to participate in yet another MOVIExperience, or to give feedback. He's always pushing the envelope, pushing, pushing.

So, I got to see where I close down and what happens when I go beyond my comfort level, what opens up. It's like these sound barriers that get broken, opening a whole world on the other side that has not been accessible, because I've been operating in the safe zone. And I guess part of it is that I trusted him and I took the ride.

Nancy Fletcher founded the nonprofit ActNow! Inc., which uses MOVIExperience to build character and confidence in people—especially women.

Nikhil Melnechuk

Student moviemaker Nikhil Melnechuk talks with David Shepherd about his techniques for making and showing low-cost movies.

David: I remember when you did your first movie two or three years ago. You had a cast of six people in a scenario, and a woman objected that you couldn't do a movie with no sound. Is that right?

Nikhil: Yeah, that's true. We had about six people. We wanted to do a story without dialogue and see if we can tell the story just with the visual aspects of moviemaking, which I'm really interested in. I like running the camera and setting up the shots and getting good lighting.

D: Did any of the cast think it was possible?

N: Some of the cast were skeptical at first. But the method works. The story was pretty simple: a robbery taking place at 2 a.m. Without dialogue, we were able to get nuances of the characters just from their looks.

D: How did you approach your last movie, "Manilla?"

N: Completely differently. I spent about three months writing a full script. It consisted mainly of dialogue with fewer stage directions than standard scripts. Then I had an open audition with about forty people. I cast about ten. I did fundraising and then started shooting.

D: Who provided funds?

N: I got a donation for about $500 from a novelist named Ken Conway. And, we held a car wash that made $600-700. And, then we had a film festival which made about $500-600.

D: Where did you get the films from?

N: From people all over town: college students, Amherst residents who are amateur video makers, and high-school students.

D: Original works?

N: Yeah, 20 original works. It was amazing. We put a notice in the paper and 500-600 posters around town, and people came out for it.

D: Good. So, where did the idea come from for "Manilla?"

N: Well, the movie is partially based on my own life experiences. I've always wanted to make a movie, I'm always thinking about ideas for a story. I wanted to find a story that resonated with me so I could really put my all into the project. I decided to write a story that would help me figure out things in a therapeutic way.

D: So what was it about the story that resonated?

N: The friendship between the two male leads and also the concept of being trapped in relationships and about how dishonesty and lying can really hurt people.

D: What's your next movie going to be about?

N: I'm not sure. I'm working on a short, 3-minute film right now. It's shot in a hotel, and there is one continuous dolly shot that pans across about twenty hotel rooms where each door is open. And, the camera lingers on each room for about fifteen seconds.

In each room, you see a really different and dramatic scene taking place, like a fight between a mother and a daughter or a man beating a woman. And, even though there is a different theme happening in each room, the dialogue is continuous from room to room. So, if you listen to the whole movie with your eyes closed, you perceive a different story than if you actually watch the movie.

And, the story that it tells is about a boy, a young and popular member of the community, who dies in a car accident. The story is slowly told and then the camera turns back on itself to the ghost of the boy who died. So, the concept is that a death in a town or family can be an underlying force.

D: I think that will be a big hit at the festivals. How does improvisation help you to make movies?

N: Although "Manilla" was scripted, improvisation definitely helped me in my directing, because I learned that actors are best when they are given room to be spontaneous. For instance, each shot probably requires between 10 and 20 takes. Although you always seem to think that the first couple takes are usually the best, with the ones afterwards going downhill, I found that the opposite was true.

The first couple of takes were very dry, because people were still ironing out dialogue problems and finding their voice in the words. Then, I did a few takes where I let the actors play around with the lines and just get into the scripts. And, then I did a few really serious takes, following the script very closely. And then, I tell the actors to play the scene in a different way than from what they have been doing.

By that point, the lines are all perfectly memorized and the actors are so into their characters that they are able to take the scene completely outside of the box. I ended up using final takes a lot. So, there was definitely a lot of improvisation.

D: Were there any surprises for you? Were there any departures from the script?

N: There were a lot: funny lines that were added or lines that were said in a different way that made them funnier. Also, one time we realized the script, as written, would not work, so we ended up changing it completely.

Or, unintentional things happen that turn out to be even better than what was scripted. For instance, there was one scene where the character is supposed to say, "It is better to have loved and lost than never to have loved at all." But, he ends up saying, "It is better to have loved a lot..." and it turned out to be very funny and I couldn't improve on that.

NOTE: "Manilla" was accepted at the Northampton Film Festival. Nikhil is a sophomore at Wesleyan College. He and his friends appear on the cover.

Glossary

Action: The physical elements that a particular scene possesses.

Analog: Audio/video signals currently being used in broadcasting where a signal is represented by variable measurable physical quantities (like voltage).

A-roll and B-roll: Procedure to collect action on one tape and on the other cutaways, locations shots, and special effects. The Latter can be clearly faded in and out of the action.

Automatic focus: An audio signal that measures distance to the subject and adjusts the camera accordingly.

Back story: Details from a character's past that justify her or his behavior now.

Barn doors: A light with 4 panels that can open or close, giving direction to the illumination.

Battery types: the type of battery that is compatible with a particular camera.

Beat: A unit of action in a scene which is made up of series of beats. "The girl comes home at 3 a.m." is a beat.

Control track: Controls vertical and horizontal in the TV picture, also called synch.

Countdown: counting out loud the number of seconds till the camera records, beginning with 5. Usually, the words "3," "2," "1," and "zero" are not voiced.

CU (Close-up): A tight shot that is generally of a player's face; face and neck; or face, neck, and shoulders.

Cut: Turning the camcorder to pause. This indicates that the next scene takes place in the same location and time frame.

Cutaway: A shot, usually a close-up of some detail joining a scene or interview that has been cut. Often a very useful editing tool; inserting it justifies continuity. Usually cutaways relate to the scene.

Degradation: Reduction in tape quality through wear or weather (heat, moisture).

Denial: When improviser plays "Yes, But" instead of "Yes, And." If you say, "Let's have coffee," and I don't respond, I'm denying you.

Digital: A system of recording based on strings of numbers where all numbers are either zero or one.

Dropout: In digital recording, clustered squares showing wear on surface of emulsion. In analog, horizontal white lines.

Dupe: Duplicate copy of a tape.

ECU (Extreme close-up): A shot where the player or subject is tight in the frame of the camera and fills the entire screen, which conveys an atmosphere of intimacy and reveals details.

EDL (Edit decision list): A list of in points and out points by which video is edited.

Fade out/fade in: A transitional device where the last image of one scene fades to black as the first image of the next scene is gradually illuminated. Implies that time has passed since the last scene or action is shifting to a new location.

Feature: An original work about ninety minutes in length that has titles, credits, pictures, sounds, and usually a story or a group of stories strung together.

Frame: A single image (out of a series of images) on a piece of film or tape.

FPS (Frames per second): The number of frames that one sees during 1 second of film being played. There are 24 frames per second.

Gain: The level of amplification of an audio or video signal.

Gel: Gelatin used to change the color of a source light.

Generation loss: Loss in quality from copying an analog video from tape to tape. Does not occur with digital video formats. A source tape is first generation, and successive dupes are second and third generation, etc.

Give and take: Players take turns giving away leadership of the scene and taking it back.

Gofer: The person who fetches what's needed to keep the moviemaking going.

Head: The beginning of a tape.

Hot spot: Light or shiny areas in the camera view that draw unwarranted focus in the scene.

Improvise: Moving from one fixed point to another while justifying your change in emotion; playing a game that enhances interaction between players; recreating a transaction from memory. Doing something without a script, without preparation, and/or without thinking or planning ahead.

Improvise in a group: With or without a scenario, a group can choose a relationship or event and discover it through improvisation.

Improvise a scenario: Process of brainstorming by which the ideas of a group are brought out without criticizing and stories are developed on the spot.

Improvise solo: A player who takes a suggestion from the audience to express a character or feeling is improvising solo.

Indicate: To present the outline of a feeling or behavior, such as sorrow or inebriation, without any internal justification.

Insert: A close-up of an aspect or detail of a scene; a cutaway.

Jump cut: A jarring lack of continuity between two images that have been edited out of the same footage.

L-cut: An edit in which the audio precedes the video or vice versa. This helps to make the edit less noticeable.

Over the shoulder: This is the standard two-shot commonly used in television. When two people are facing each other and conversing, the camera is over the shoulder of the actor not speaking, focused on the actor who is.

Manual focus: This is often used to reduce strain when a camera battery is low.

Mark: To keep the camera in focus, the operator of the camera must know where a player will enter or leave. The player is given marks therefore: "Go to the bed and stop. Then go to the door." The player must then improvise a reason to go to the bed, stop, and then go to the door. To make a mark, put a cross on the floor with masking tape.

MS (medium shot): A shot in a film where a character is framed from the waist, hips or knees up (or down) and the camera is amply distanced from the body, which allows the character to be viewed in relation to his or her surroundings.

Outro: The music played at the end of a movie; the opposite of intro.

Pan: A horizontal camera move on an axis, moving from right to left or from left to right, while the camera is turning on an axis.

Player: An actor.

Props: An object used on stage or in front of a camera or audience to visually enhance a scene. In stage improv, hand props are not used. (There is no real table on which to put a mug, for instance.) So, players discover the table in space as well as the mug. On camera, real props are used. Costumes may also serve as props on stage and on camera.

Scenario: A series of events or changes between people.

Scene: The verbal/physical performance and/or presentation or expression of an improv or theater game.

Script: The text of dramatic work.

Shoot in sequence/out of sequence: When you improvise the same order of scenes that's been given by the scenario, you are in sequence. If you were to shoot the last scene first, you'd be shooting out of sequence.

Special effects: Ways to edit tape such as black & white, soft image and colorization. It also includes distortion of background, sound, and voices.

Steady cam: A cradle of the camcorder in which a gyroscope steadies the hand of the camera operator.

Steamrolling: When a player racks up his energy and pushes other players around.

Storyboard: A series of key images sketched to suggest what a series of shots will look like.

Swish pan: A very fast pan taking in an area of the location with no detail.

Take: A recording from the countdown to where action is cut.

Talent release: Gives the producer permission to dupe, distribute, or sell footage in which the subject appears. Cable stations are often strict about getting releases signed by both child and parent.

Tech: The technical aspects of moviemaking, such as lighting, sound, and editing.

Text: The opposite of improv; text dictates exactly what is to be said or done, while improv offers the opportunity to discover.

Tilt: A vertical camera move on an axis, either moving up or moving down.

Video: Means half-inch VHS for cable TV and local screenings.

Video heads: Tiny sensors that spin over the surface of the video tape, bringing an image to the screen. When the heads are dirty this process is compromised.

White balance: An element of the camera control that adjusts color sensitivity (either automatically or manually). Circuitry is adjusted to the color temperature of a lighting source so that white object is rendered as white when viewed on screen.

Yes...And: A game that prohibits denial. Players must build on each other's choices and offerings.

Zoom in/out: Brings the subject closer to you, or makes it appear that you are moving away.

Bibliography

Books

Burns, Michael. *First You Sit on the Floor: Guide to Developing a Youth Theatre Troupe*, Heinemann: 2002.

Close, Del, Halpern, Charna, Johnson, Kim Howard, and Myers, Mike. *Truth in Comedy: The Manual of Improvisation*. Meriwether Pub; 1st edition: 1994.

Coleman, Janet. The Compass: The Improvisational Theatre that Revolutionized American Comedy, Knopf: 1990.

Johnstone, Keith. *Impro*, Methuen Drama: 1998.

Johnstone, Keith. *Impro for Storytellers*, Routledge Theatre Arts Books: 1999.

Kneelands, Jonathan, Goode, Tony. *Structuring Drama Work*, Cambridge University Press: 2000.

Gesell, Izzy. *Playing Along: 37 Group Learning Activities Based on Improvisational Theatre*, Whole Person Associates: 1997.

Goldberg, Andy. *Improv Comedy*. Samuel French Trade: 1992.

Nevraumont, Edward J.; Hanson, Nicholas P.; Smeaton, Kurt. *The Ultimate Improv Book: A Complete Guide to Comedy Improvisation*, Meriwether Pub: January, 2002.

Rohd, Michael. *Theater for Community Conflict and Dialogue*, Heinemann: 1998.

Seham, Amy. *Whose Improv Is It Anyway?: Beyond Second City*, Mississippi University Press: 2001.

Spolin, Viola. *Improvisation for the Theater: A Handbook of Teaching and Directing Techniques*. Northwestern University Press; 3rd edition: July, 1999.

Sweet, Jeff. *Something Wonderful Right Away: An Oral History of the Second City and The Compass Players*, Limelight Editions: May, 1987.

Independent Movies

Slackers
Clerks
El Mariachi
Women Under the Influence (any film by John Cassavetes)
Naked
Any movie by Christopher Guest

Film/Video Sound Websites

http://www.filmsound.org
http://www.dolby.com
http://www.fsfl.home.se/tips.html
http://www.dilettantesdictionary.com

Acknowledgments

I want to thank Claudia Gere for taking on this project, which had been stacked for years on the carpet of Mark Siska and others wandering into the orbit of Group Create.

Nancy Fletcher did me the honor of activating MOVIExperience at the other end of the spectrum—with 12-year-old girls. Like a Research Project turned real.

Mike DiPaolo repeated for years: "You have a gold mine, David. Just do your thing for wealthy people and be sure to address their feelings. Their Experience."

During the weeks leading up to Labor Day 2003, Jackie di Chiara took care of a dozen issues from Casting Players to researching a national magazine article.

Jack Tannenbaum passed my manuscript pages through the eye of several needles going one way, and David Chase passed them back.

A lot of people had something to say—in the book. And actually said it. A few friends felt close enough to the project to shape it: Karl Benko, David Brager, Dan Sutherland, John McCluskey, Howard Jerome, and Michael Golding.

A few people actually read the manuscript: among them Hope 0' Shaughnessy, David Lutzer & Jeff Metzger; while Vic Teich gave fast answers to questionable paragraphs.

Izzy Gesell and Philip Belove, New England's paraconscious gurus, also fit into our scheme, somehow or other, day or night.

As did my son, Evan with his gift for TrueFine.

As did other designers, trainers, musicians, editors . . .

This list also includes those whose name will occur to me a few minutes after I flick these fervent thanks into the electronic cauldron—for publication throughout the universe.

The Author

Index

About the Author

David Shepherd produced the first professional improv cabaret theater in America, Chicago COMPASS, which evolved into Second City, launching the careers of masters such as Jerry Stiller, Mike Nichols, Alan Alda, Barbara Harris, Elaine May, Ed Asner, and Shelly Berman. Most recently he was presented with lifetime achievement awards by Canadian Improv Games and Chicago Improv Fest for his pioneering roles.

According to Alan Arkin, "David Shepherd is the Johnnie Appleseed of improv." David not only conceived and produced the first professional theatre of improv, he also invented or shaped over nine other improv formats, including Novella, Radio, Movie, Performance Sport, ImprovOlympix, Other Selves, Video Holiday, Poetry Games, and Video Scape. David leads improv workshops and creates video movies with amateurs and professionals throughout North America: Winnipeg, Toronto, Ottawa, the Hamptons, NYC, Boston, and Western Massachusetts where he lives.